To Jon Daily and Angela Chanter, your mentorship and friendship have impacted my mind and life in ways that I could not have foreseen. I am forever changed by knowing you, and for that I am unabashedly grateful.

To my father, whose wisdom and encouragement afforded me the courage to tell the truth to help others along their journey in life.

To all those who are struggling, your pain is real but you *can* overcome it with time, effort, and change.

www.mascotbooks.com

*The Fear Problem: How Technology and Culture Have
Hijacked Our Minds and Lives*

For more information, please contact:
Mascot Books
620 Herndon Parkway, Suite 320
Herndon, VA 20170
info@mascotbooks.com

Library of Congress Control Number: 2018903297

CPSIA Code: PRBVG0718A
ISBN-13: 978-1-68401-813-0

Printed in the United States

THE
FEAR
PROBLEM

How Technology and Culture Have
Hijacked Our Minds and Lives

Dr. Patrick Lockwood

A Note from the Author

I grew up in a small southern Missouri town and eventually moved to southern California to pursue my doctorate in psychology after finishing my undergraduate studies at the University of Missouri. Since I've been living in Los Angeles, I have come to appreciate how culturally diverse and complex relationships can be, which has greatly influenced how I negotiate both clinical and business relationships. These experiences have convinced me to advocate for the most integrative approach to problem-solving with my clients, because life is terribly complex.

Growing up in a community where addiction, economic struggles, and prejudice were commonplace, I find that I have a strong sense of empathy for how stuck, powerless, or unaccepted a person can feel. I believe it is my purpose in life to try to help individuals, communities, and organizations become free from such emotional hindrances so they can develop clarity about their direction and purpose, and ultimately succeed.

Preface

In the past 50 years the social, political, and technological landscape of the world has changed dramatically. These changes have left a mark on us and our ability to maintain our peace of mind. Moreover, we face even greater challenges as our understanding of what it means to be human and coexist evolves. This book can hopefully serve as a conversation starter for all of us about how, despite significant improvements in the quality of life for many, it seems like we still struggle a great deal to feel safe and have fulfilling lives as we move throughout our day.

This book, *The Fear Problem*, explores the psychological and social landscape of what I see to be one of our most fundamental struggles to live and succeed—managing fear. As it is with all treatises focusing on the human condition, what follows are a variety of educated assumptions about human behavior and societal functioning.

This work is not meant to function like a self-help book or an opinion piece in a newspaper. What I've attempted to do is craft a narrative, a conversation, that explores how our most primal instinctual response (i.e., fear) has both served us greatly and is now—theoretically—acting as a hindrance to our progress and wellbeing.

It is my sincere hope that we can have many discussions going forward about the nature of being human and how our emotional process works both for us and against us, and why that's so. Despite years of scientific advancement in the fields of medicine, neuroscience, psychology, and sociology, much is still up for debate about what is "healthy" or optimal when it comes to expressing and managing our feelings. With any luck this work can help all of us think more critically about how we think we "work" and where to focus our debate in the future.

DR. PATRICK LOCKWOOD

TABLE OF CONTENTS

> "This world of ours... must avoid becoming a
> community of dreadful fear and hate, and be, instead,
> a proud confederation of mutual trust and respect."
>
> **DWIGHT D. EISENHOWER**

INTRODUCTION

The Problem

F ear: Perhaps the most primal emotion animals experience. Most individuals experience some degree of fear about the various events occurring throughout the day. Perhaps you felt fear today when you went to work because you were concerned about a deadline or project. Or, maybe you were in a threatening situation in traffic when someone changed lanes without looking. With all the wars and conflicts occurring at present, it's highly likely that thousands of soldiers, combatants, and civilian bystanders are experiencing strong fear at this very moment. There are hundreds of circumstances in which we all feel fear, and for good reason—I propose. Without fear, and other emotions, humans and other extant animal species would not have survived.

Ask yourself a question: what would be the most likely emotional driving force in many of our social, political, economic, personal, and religious practices? Hope?

No, I don't think so because the tone of our discourse is not typically optimistic or pleasant, but usually warier. The number of wars, jihads, disease epidemics, political conflicts, and discussions about social unrest have increased in the last 200 years. Watch any political debate in most Western countries like the United States and you will hear candidates for positions at every level of government making speeches about how bad their opponent will be for you, your family, and your livelihood.

Go to any primary, secondary, or postsecondary educational institution and you will undoubtedly find bullying, strong academic competition, and/or "cliques." Ask most CEOs of major corporations, as well as small businesses, about their financial or development goals for the coming fiscal year and I guarantee that these leaders will say something along the lines of wanting market growth or increased profits. Watch news videos of religious extremists of almost any faith and you will hear them scream, use hate speech, act violently, and/or just warn others about the dangers of some apocalypse or group of people.

These are all fear-driven dynamics. Just playing it by the numbers, if you read the fifth edition of the American Psychiatric Association's *Diagnostic and Statistical Manual of Mental Disorders*, (i.e., the Western world's fully sanctioned bible of mental problems), you would find that the prevalence of anxiety-related disorders in the general population sits somewhere between 8 and 15 percent of the general population. Fear runs rampant throughout multiple sectors of our lives.

The immensity of our fear responses can easily be seen in the ghastly political climate of the United States. If we take, for example, the 2016 U.S. presidential election campaign, it is painfully obvious that the mudslinging, name-calling, and conspiracy theories were driven by some relatively unrealistic fear that the country will be "ruined" if this or that candidate wins the election and some stupidly optimistic belief that one candidate or the other could "fix" the problems of our country.

From Donald Trump being cast as a racist, bigot, nationalist, and generally belligerent narcissist, to Hillary Clinton being described as a heartless, resentful globalist who's so politically desperate that she is a shill for the banking industry and foreign interests, both sides of the aisle worked their hardest to instill fear in the American people with the help of the news media. This past election was perhaps one of the most vitriolic in the last 100 years, which can only mean people were struggling with a great deal of fear about the future of the country. Looking back on it now, it seems like the depths of despair, fear, and paranoia in 2016 could not have been rivaled by anything in recent history except for the attack on the U.S. that occurred on September 11th, 2001 or, further back, the peak of the Cold War threat of nuclear war with Russia.

How about events we all might consider very positive? The invention of a vaccine by Jonas Salk revolutionized medicine. The creation of a non-profit business focused on helping veterans reintegrate into society and heal after valiantly serving their country is very touching. The profound and socially-valued experience of a couple getting married seems wonderful. Writing a book to help people learn, grow, and change is an act of care and concern. Religious individuals waking up in the morning and praying for peace and resolution must be all too common an example.

How about our use of modern technology like cellular phones, tablets, and social media? Imagine receiving a text message or tweet from a friend, lover, or coworker. I bet you feel an urge to respond right away because you have become accustomed to the rapid pace associated with the world's amazing technological advancements. These all seem like very positive and valuable experiences in which people engage daily. The world is rapidly changing, and for good reason.

But what is it that drives all of these individuals to act or respond as they do in the aforementioned examples? Fear. We could, however, argue for hours, days, weeks, months, and years about the cultural, economic, logistical, intellectual, and other factors that likely influence anyone in the examples above, but that would not be fruitful for the purposes of getting to the bottom line as I see it.

Regardless of any of the hundreds of variables that can influence people to say or do things reactively or proactively, the fundamental truth that I hope to convince you of in the following pages is that our fear, our universal primal drive to survive and succeed, is the one variable that has become a problem in not only Western and Middle Eastern cultures, but the world over. Advancements in technology, medicine, communication, and a boundless number of social rights groups the world over are great examples of how our proactive-reactive responses to fear have impacted the world in a more positive direction. Our fear response has been hijacked, leaving us constantly on the alert, and we need to take back control over our emotional destiny.

Premises

The hallmark of any good argument is that it has clear, easily discernable points that can be supported with facts and other compelling forms of evidence. Therefore, in the following section I would like to outline my arguments for why I believe individuals, sub-cultures, and societies have allowed their unchecked fear to become an unfortunate driving force in many of their behaviors and decisions.

I want to re-emphasize the "unchecked" part of my last statement. Fear is a normal, biologically-based reaction that cannot be simply eradicated, with the exception of the destruction of our amygdala and associated emotional brain structures (1, 2). We need fear, as noted above. The problem, however, is that, for reasons to be explained in later chapters, we have all become more reactive and allowed ourselves to get hijacked by our fear. Later, I will discuss some reasons as to why we're more reactive, such as the increased speed of communication and profound growth of information and interpersonal contact.

So, the first premise that I hope to prove in this book is that our fear is a necessity, but that it is slowly growing out of control *in unnoticeable ways*. To prove this point, I will be drawing on writings, research, and examples from many academic and media sources. On a daily basis, our fear prompts us to engage in activities and behaviors that allow us to eat, function, succeed, and survive.

In the last 200 years, the conditions we live in and our means of survival (literally and socially) have changed. Because our conditions of survival have changed, I believe **our relationship with fear needs to change**. So, I wish to make it ultimately clear that the goal of this book, and this specific premise, is not to show that our biological programming is a bad thing. Quite the contrary, in fact, the hope is that some of my arguments throughout this book will actually leverage your fear to promote change in a more positive direction!

The second premise that I hope to prove in this book is that our unchecked fear, both in an individual sense and our behavior in larger groups (i.e., culture, country, or ideology), to some degree or another has become one of the most destructive forces for us all. I intend to show proof for how unchecked fear has become a destructive force on three levels.

First, I intend to offer evidence that unchecked fear has a destructive impact on the individual and for many areas of their life. Second, I hope to prove empirically that unchecked fear in any and all cultures has a destructive impact for that culture. Finally, I intend to leverage the first two levels of proof to show how various individuals' and cultures' unchecked fear has had a fundamentally damaging impact on world politics, social practices, and health.

For example, looking at the current geopolitical landscape, the U.S. and many other countries are engaged in military conflicts, but why? Fear. We fight for our survival; we fight to maintain our sense of safety and stability. The emotion driving these fights is fear. You don't have to look any further than recent news headlines to find an intense rhetoric between Kim Jong Un, the leader of North Korea, who threatened the U.S. with nuclear war, and President Donald Trump to see perhaps the most obvious example of attempting to stave off a fear response to a threat to survival. You may have even had an argument with a friend or loved one about how Donald Trump "should" be handling North Korea.

Moreover, you could easily say that the emotional reason for the ongoing wars in the Middle East with ISIS and their predecessors is the national and international fear reaction after the attacks here on September 11, 2001. What could be more dangerous and life-threatening than a terrorist group that wishes to destroy not only a country, but more so the "Western" way of living? This shows how fear can create consequences for everyone at pretty much every level of societal functioning.

The final premise I hope to prove in this book is that, although there are seemingly obvious or simple solutions to managing, diminishing, or re-focusing our fear (solutions I'll offer), the challenges we face as individuals and cultures to actually choose to live life differently and check our fear are too great. We will likely not change anytime soon, or at all, unless drastic and concerted efforts are undertaken.

I'm certain this sounds cynical, and it partly is because what I propose is that we have to make a choice to live life differently. Major changes, personally or socially, take years or even decades. Based upon my work as a therapist and consultant, I can attest to the fact that significant individual change takes a long time. Therefore, on top of the likely bleak outlook, I hope to prove that we need to learn how to be patient with ourselves, our friends and intimate others, our culture, our governments, and our world climate.

As I stated, I intend to offer at the end of this work a few potential solutions for how to better check our fear. On an individual level, there are dozens of physical, mental, interpersonal, and lifestyle ideas that can be offered to help manage fear in the moment, as well as decrease the likelihood of living a more fear-based lifestyle, appropriate to your given context.

For instance, simple changes in exercise and the addition of wellness-based practices like meditation can help decrease an individual's average daily experience of anxiety (i.e., fear) significantly. More drastic individual efforts (i.e., therapy, medications, and major lifestyle changes) may be needed if you more strongly experience anxiety on a daily basis. On a cultural level, there are fewer ideas or insights I can offer the world because sociology and politics are disciplines I am not trained in, and I have no desire to misrepresent my capabilities—though I intend to attempt to offer sound and logical propositions for culture-group fear checking.

The truth is the many cultural, social, religious, political, and other ways we group ourselves are recalcitrant. There is a great deal of rigidity among religious individuals, for example. Pick a major ideology, like Christianity, and you will find that various types of Christians believe other kinds "don't have it right" and are therefore going to hell—arguing and fighting intensely with others about the "truth." This is a dynamic on display in the Middle East today, where factions of Islam (e.g., Sunni versus Shia) have been warring for the past 2,000 years. I propose that the rigidity and bellicose nature of cultural division is due to the fact that these groups are composed of individuals.

Individuals are flawed and ironically, afraid to change. Moreover, the level of hypocrisy in any of the aforementioned groups has yet to be addressed, probably out of fear. Hypocrisy is another factor that plays into the recalcitrance of the cultural fear problem. On a global scale, I believe the solutions and discussions about how to help cultures change will play a major part in helping the world check their fear-based policies. Again, I am not a sociologist by training, and I do not consider myself a religious or political scholar. Ergo, I have no vested interest in "changing the world." My hope is to convince you to have a more mindful attitude towards your fear experiences and how you deal with moments of being hijacked by your emotions.

Final Thoughts

I want to conclude this introductory chapter by challenging your perspective on learning and then your perspective on living. Regardless of your age, culture, occupation, level of education, political affiliation, religious beliefs, or any other self-identifying characteristics, please try to suspend your preconceived beliefs, biases, and previous learning.

I challenge you to read the remainder of this book with an open mind, what academics call "transformative learning." There is a fundamental difference between reading something and thinking, "Oh, this conflicts with what I believe or how I was raised, so I'm not going to give it a chance" *versus* "Well, what this writer is saying makes me uncomfortable and challenges my beliefs, but maybe it's a good thing and I can learn from what I'm reading." I hope that you choose the latter way of approaching this text, which will make the next few statements I make more tolerable I hope.

Freud once wrote in *Civilization and its Discontents*, "The fateful question for the human species seems to me to be whether and to what extent their cultural development will succeed in mastering the disturbance of their communal life by the human instinct of aggression and self-destruction" (3). Freud here appears to be discussing what psychoanalysts call "annihilation anxiety," which can generally be described as our instinctual fear of dying, present at birth.

This fear pushes us to fight (i.e., a reactive defense against anxiety) or achieve (i.e., a proactive defense to prevent anxiety). One way to interpret Freud's words would be to say that people will not advance or evolve so long as we succumb to our annihilation anxiety (i.e., instinctive fear of death). In fact, as Freud predicts, the more we succumb to our fear of dying, the more it results in destructive acts.

Let's take a quick look back at recent world events again. Based on the events in August 2016, it occurs to me that Freud was right. The Western

World's fear of death, attack, or loss of power can be readily seen in all the conflicts with ISIS, Iran, North Korea, Russia, China, and about 80 other powers or groups that also seem to be reacting and proactively behaving due to strong fear. In fact, an article a few years ago in *The Nation* found sources evidencing that the United States alone had special forces in over 133 countries, which represents an 80 percent increase compared to roughly five years ago (4).

The widespread fear and international conflict is both exasperating and scary. Looking back 100 years in history, the sheer number of global, country-destroying conflicts, was at least tenfold less. But…why? Again, as Freud said, our cultures—despite profound advances in technology and medicine—have not truly evolved past our more primitive instincts. I believe we have not evolved past our more primitive instincts. I believe we typically choose not to better manage our primitive instincts, because our primitive instincts/emotions still can and do serve us to proactively work for a better individual and collective life. This is a point I will more thoroughly discuss in the next chapter.

So, the world is at war, has there not always been international conflict? The correct answer is "Well, yes of course." It is entirely likely that this lifestyle of fear many individuals and cultures have adopted will not change significantly, or at least not without some major catalyst. There is another problem with this desire for "big change" in the world.

Peace is not a possibility. From a biological, historical, and evolutionary perspective, there is no proof that humans and other animals have ever been at peace consistently, nor were we/they designed for complete peace. The non-possibility of peace will also be covered in the next couple chapters. Ergo, if none of us are designed to be at peace, then why should we expect the world to be at peace?

It seems as if Darwin's argument, that survival is all we strive for and the fittest survive the longest or in the best way (5), is appropriate here. If you believe Darwin's theory–that our internal drive for survival and drive to attain fitness for better survival over our peers leads to normal and expectable conflict *as well as* loving cooperation– then peace is definitely not a possibility.

In fact, I believe it to be profoundly inane and infantile when any scholar, politician, philosopher, or group of people push for world peace or sustained peace in some land. Asking humans to not be *human* is likely a failed strategy and a waste of words. Even though humans are the most evolved species in the mammalian group, we're still primal creatures with a need to survive and thrive.

I would like to make a more philosophical note and distinction for anyone who has read thus far and feels concerned about what I seem to be espousing about the "solution" to the fear problem. This is not some kind of Communist or Marxist manifesto. I do not believe we all need to be reorganizing society and singing "Kumbaya." It would be delusional to believe that the unattainably idealistic notions of any socialist conceptions in ideologies like Communism or Marxism have any chance of working as their original authors hoped for, because, again, our Darwinist (i.e., fear-driven) desire to succeed and survive should always promote some amount of expectable, manageable, and productive competition towards a better life.

This is a concept exemplified in the normal curve. A certain percentage of the population will struggle a significant amount by chance or by failing to thrive. Some people will be born in disadvantageous biological or social circumstances. Whereas others will by chance and/or by effort be more advantaged.

Roughly 68 percent of us will live in the middle in terms of fitness, attractiveness, intelligence, wealth, education, and comfort taken together as an aggregate. Naturally so, people will strive to better themselves to get towards the second and third standard deviation on the normal curve regarding any of these concepts. This concept has been suspiciously absent from the fight about the "one percent" in terms of wealth here in the U.S.

It would be positively incredulous to propose challenging others to completely deny their instincts towards becoming "better than you" as a socialist ideology would ask us to do. This has no chance of succeeding for any length of time in large groups. Life in general, and more specifically individual psychological functioning, is too complex a concept to afford us the ability to pick one ideology as all encompassing. For further arguments to support this point listen to the talks given by speakers like Dr. Jordan Peterson.

It is, therefore, the goal of this work to inform, convince, and challenge you, the reader, and make clear the insidious and destructive changes that have occurred due to our unchecked fear—both individually and in various social and cultural groups. The secondary goal of this work is to help the reader find more ways to understand and manage both personal fear issues and how each individual reader contributes to the propagation or diminishment of the fear narrative and operations in their society and cultural groups. Finally, and most practicably, it is my hope that we can begin to have discussions in our homes, with our friends, at our political conventions, places of business, and everywhere else about the truth, the truth about what we as individuals and groups desire most.

If any of us were to be completely honest about the most important goals we have, then we would find that fear is at least partly responsible for them. The problem is simple: our healthy fear has been hijacked by our lifestyles and cultures and become the impetus for many significant problems in our lives as individuals and groups.

REFERENCES

---

1.   Weiskrantz, L. (1956). Behavioral changes associated with ablation of the amygdaloid complex in monkeys. *Journal of Comparative and Physiological Psychology, 49*(4), 381-391.

2.   Emery, N. J., Capitanio, J. P., Mason, W. A., Machado, C.J.; Mendoza, S.P.; Amaral, D. G. (2001). The effects of bilateral lesions of the amygdala on dyadic social interactions in rhesus monkeys (*Macaca mulatta*). *Behavioral Neuroscience, 115*(3), Jun 2001, 515-544. http://dx.doi.org/10.1037/0735-7044.115.3.515

3.   Freud, S. (1930). *Civilization and its discontents.* (Trans. James Strachey, 2010). New York, NY: W.W. Norton & Sons.

4.   Turse, N. (2015). How many wars is the U.S. really fighting? The Nation. Retrieved on August 7th, 2016 from: https://www.thenation.com/article/how-many-wars-is-the-us-really-fighting/

5.   Darwin, Charles (1872), "The Origin of Species by Means of Natural Selection, or the Preservation of Favoured Races in the Struggle for Life," *Nature* (6th ed.), London: John Murray.

> "We can easily forgive a child who is afraid of the dark; the real tragedy of life is when men are afraid of the light."
>
> **PLATO**

CHAPTER 1:
TYPES OF FEAR

A Psychological Approach

Over the last 100 or so years, authors, practitioners, and researchers within psychology and related disciplines have been discussing how to conceptualize fear and anxiety. Again, for the sake of simplicity, I'm going to separate out the less pertinent details of fear research and focus on the predominant paradigms. The next chapter is going to discuss the biological mechanisms that underlie what we describe as fear in our everyday discussions.

For now, I'd like to differentiate between the two predominant kinds of fear reactions we experience from a psychological standpoint: "innate" fear and "learned" fear. As you'll learn by reading on in this chapter, the descriptions of these two types of fear seem somewhat self-explanatory, but the differences are deceptively simple in terms of how one type of fear or another is problematic. Once you read on into the next chapter about the biological forces at play in our fear circuitry, it will become even more clear how obvious yet insidious our fear process works to both help us function and survive, as well as lead to problems discussed in chapters 4 through 7.

Instinctual Fear

A uthors across many scientific disciplines group fear into two categories: instinctual fear and learned fear (1-3). The first type of fear, instinctual fear, is found in all humans, mammals, and most reptiles. We are all programmed to be afraid of people or experiences that can harm our ability to thrive, survive, or satisfy other basic evolutionary needs.

This innate fear response comes in two varieties. First, we will all naturally have a fear response whenever we perceive our physical wellbeing is being threatened. For example, research using different species of animals shows that they will become afraid of predator pheromones even if the animal has never been exposed to the predator (3). This shows that there is an inherited schema or model in these animal brains for "Oh, I sense this predator chemical, I should be afraid and act accordingly." Moreover, research shows that humans innately scan faces and automatically feel afraid when we perceive a threatening or fearful facial expression (4).

This kind of research and other commonly accepted scientific assertions point to an evolutionary need for an innate fear of varying levels of threatening circumstances or individuals. Other common examples of instinctually-based fears are reactions to dangerous animals, insects, and bodily states (e.g., choking, extreme pain, sight of blood, etc.).

Second, we all have innate fear responses related to being socially disconnected from or by important others in our presence. Essentially, we all have an evolutionarily necessity to be supported by and connected to people (5-10). From the moment we are born to the moment we die, we are all seeking connection. Connection with others helps us feel safe, survive better, and develop a ready source of "mirroring" (i.e., empathic relating) and support for our needs.

Because we need connection, from less intense connections like acquaintances or passersby on the street to more intense connections like the bond between lovers or parents and their children, we naturally feel afraid when we perceive that we are losing a connection (i.e., separation anxiety). Generally, the intensity of the connection with the person will dictate the intensity of the fear response when someone attempts to, or actually does, separate from us. After we are separated, we typically feel sad or ashamed (6, 7). So, to clarify, I'm only focusing here on the perception of separation from people in our lives.

Generally speaking, our innate fears should not result in many problematic consequences. If you think about the last time you saw a spider while walking around your neighborhood or on a hike, you probably had a feeling of fear that encouraged you to move away from it, or maybe even kill it. Theoretically, this response you had, which all of us have had, is not going to result in any negative consequences. At worst, we might trip as we run away. There are, however, some instances where our innate fear response might become problematic in modern day life.

The simplest example is driving. Driving is a learned behavior. Our more primitive ancestors had no cars, so we have no biological schemata for driving. We do, however, have an innate fear response related to large objects coming at us—especially if said large object is out of control or unavoidable. This would be akin to the fear a monkey might feel when a rhinoceros is stampeding in its general direction. So, when we drive nowadays, we are surrounded by numerous large, out-of-control objects.

Now and again, or almost every day if you're in Los Angeles like myself, we might experience a careless driver swerving into our lane or not paying attention and almost hitting us as we drive. When this happens, we often feel a fear or possibly a "rage" response and we might even feel compelled to "flip the bird" in the direction of the car threatening us. This can be problematic because it can result in other accidents or possibly even fights on the road (i.e., road rage), which is sadly a somewhat common experience in big cities all over the world.

This is an example of how a direct threat to our survival, an innate fear response, can lead to negative consequences and maladaptive behaviors. Again, I emphatically assert that our natural "gut" (i.e., innate) response of fear is not typically problematic.

Learned Fear

The second kind of fear—learned fear—is born out of the process of capitalizing on or modifying our instinctual fear response. When we are exposed to situations, persons, places, or things that directly, or are related to an experience that, elicits our innate fear response we then "learn"—via direct activation of the same innate fear brain pathways—to fear that once neutral situation, person, place, or thing (11). Researchers in psychology typically call this process "fear conditioning" or "fear learning." (12).

The first well-known example of learned fear comes from John Watson's torturing a baby named "Little Albert" by teaching him to be afraid of seemingly cute animals (13)—feel free to check out the videos on YouTube. No person is inherently (i.e., from birth) afraid of a cute looking white rabbit, but Little Albert was after Watson finished teaching him to associate a loud, scary, unexpected noise with seeing a white rabbit.

So, let's use the Little Albert example of learned fears in the context of gun violence. This will probably cause some of you to get a little upset, so try to bear with me. I'm not advocating for gun control or a gun free-for-all, so calm down. This is purely an academic thought experiment regarding how learned fear occurs in humans and most animals.

Take any 6-month-old infant and place them in a room with nothing in it except one toy the infant has never seen or played with before and a handgun, let's say an *unloaded* Glock 9mm for the sake of this example. I guarantee you that the majority of infants around this age will readily explore both the toy and the handgun, with both equal reservation and curiosity. Why? Because infants know only to fear persons, places, things, or situations that trigger their instinctual fear (i.e., is this safe or unsafe?).

Let's say, theoretically, you load the gun and fire off said handgun unexpectedly in front of (not at) the infant. After only one unexpected firing, I can also guarantee the infant will cry, have hearing problems, be afraid of the gun, and it will probably avoid handguns in the future if put in the same theoretical room. You would also probably end up in jail for child endangerment or something of that nature. But why would the infant become essentially permanently afraid of handguns? Again, we are biologically predisposed to be afraid of loud and unexpected noises—just like in the case of Little Albert.

So, what happened was the once-neutral handgun the infant was first exposed to was "interesting" sitting in the same room with the toy. The gun then became "scary" after it was unexpectedly fired because the loud noise elicited the infant's natural shock/fear response. This example can be generalized to most phenomenon we are afraid of nowadays in the "civilized" world.

Fear of people who look seemingly like a stereotypical terrorist from the Middle East is a good example. You show a dark-skinned, bearded man in a turban holding an ISIS flag to a baby and the baby will smile and try to get his attention until the man responds to the baby's attempts by smiling or scowling. An adult from the U.S., however, would likely feel some fear/hesitation when confronted with the same figure because of the last 15 years of being exposed to the media and politicians associating stereotypically Middle Eastern-looking individuals with threats to safety. Please take care in reading the next paragraph because what I'm about to say is very important and very specifically worded.

Is this a realistic and reasonable fear for the adult? I'd say yes because Islamic extremist groups typically reside and recruit in the Middle East and Africa, wherein cultures look a certain way. Moreover, Islamic extremists have been the most destructive outside groups to attack the U.S. in the recent past. Therefore, it's reasonable to have at the very least a low-level fear response to someone fitting the stereotypical Middle Eastern profile if you've constantly been told to be afraid of and seen bad things happen at the hands of people fitting their description.

I'm not, however, asserting that we need to *succumb* to our fear and treat individuals of Middle-Eastern culture or descent with hatred, disrespect, or intense circumspection. I believe, but can't prove empirically, that it would be *fair* to say that a significant majority of stereotypically Middle Eastern-looking individuals we might meet in the U.S. are normal law-abiding individuals with no ties to dangerous groups.

Unfortunately, most people are too hijacked by their fear to take a more civil approach towards their fellow man. This example can serve in your minds as a basic template for the fear hijacking phenomenon I want to help us understand and cope with better.

Summary

This has been a brief overview of the two distinct types of fear responses all humans and animals will show when presented with a perceived threat. I want to draw special attention to the use of the word "perceived" in the last sentence because it actually is the crux of my arguments throughout this book. We all have, essentially, the same basic instinctual fears no matter where we are born, what language we speak, or how we are raised. What may differ, indeed, is how we learn to be afraid of various persons, situations, objects, or ideas.

We're discussing now a problem of perception. How we are taught to perceive things is the source of our hijacked fear phenomenon. There are many, many details and factors that go into how we learn to be afraid of these various phenomena, which I will undertake in later chapters more thoroughly when I discuss the social drivers of our fear hijacking process.

What also may differ is how we express our fear response. Some families and cultures are more verbally expressive when it comes to coping with their feelings, whereas other families and cultures might be more behaviorally inclined to express their fear. Yet some people might be so badly traumatized or shamed for expressing their feelings that they might shy away from expressing them at all. Most people learn how to express their fear in various ways.

For now, I simply want to reinforce that we are looking at a battle of learned fear. So, let's put this all together, brain and psyche, which is discussed in the next chapter.

REFERENCES

1. Panksepp, J. & Biven, L. (2012). *Archaeology of Mind: The Neuroevolutionary Origins of Human Emotions.* New York: Norton.

2. Kindt, M. (2014). A behavioural neuroscience perspective on the aetiology and treatment of anxiety disorders. *Behaviour Research and Therapy, 62,* 24-36.

3. Panksepp, J., Fuchs, T., & Iacobucci, P. (2011). The basic neuroscience of emotional experiences in mammals: The case of subcortical FEAR circuitry and implications for clinical anxiety. *Applied Animal Behaviour Science,*129(1), 1-17.

4. Adolphs, R. (2008). Fear, faces, and the human amygdala. *Current Opinion in Neurobiology, 18*(2), 166-172.

5. Bowlby, J. (1969), *Attachment and loss, Vol. 1: Attachment.* New York: Basic Books.

6. Bowlby, J. (1973). *Attachment and loss, Vol. 2: Separation.* New York: Basic Books.

7. Bowlby, J. (1980). *Attachment and loss, Vol. 3: Loss, sadness and depression.* New York: Basic Books.

8. Siegel, D.J. (2012). *The developing mind, second edition: How relationships and the brain interact to shape who we are.* New York: Guilford Press.

9. Sroufe, A., & Siegel, D.J. (2011). The verdict is in: The case for attachment theory. *Psychotherapy Networker.*

10. Siegel, D.J., & Hartzell, M. (2003). *Parenting from the inside out: How a deeper self-understanding can help you raise children who thrive.* New York: Penguin Putnam.

11. Maren, S. (2001). Neurobiology of Pavlovian fear conditioning. *Annual Review of Neuroscience, 24,* 897-931.

12. Rosen, J. B. & Schulkin, J. (1998). From normal fear to pathological anxiety. *Psychological Review, 105*(2), 325-350.

13. DeAngelis, T. (2010). 'Little Albert' regains his identity. *Monitor On Psychology, 41*(1), 10. Retrieved on May 6th, 2017 from: http://www.apa.org/monitor/2010/01/little-albert.aspx

"If you know the enemy and know yourself, you need not fear the results of a hundred battles."

SUN TZU

CHAPTER 2:
BIOEVOLUTIONARY ORIGINS OF FEAR

Humans are without a doubt one of the most advanced species that exists for one basic reason: frontal and neocortex volume development. Our neocortex is the outer layer of the brain responsible for intricate processing of information in the brain.

The most advanced scientific achievements, like the Hubble telescope and cellular phone technology, as well as revolutionary moral and philosophical insights, are all due to the evolution of the neocortex— our best tool. As our higher brain areas have evolved, our societies and cultures have had to continuously update rules, politics, and relational principles in accordance with the intellectual and philosophical growth afforded by such brain evolution.

Certain parts of brain (i.e., our emotional midbrain) have not evolved in the same sophisticated way. Moreover, the way we manage our less developed emotional midbrain is still relatively...medieval. I propose that this disconnect between midbrain evolution compared to our technological and sociocultural advances prompted by forebrain/cortex evolution sits at the foundation of our fear problem in this world.

Let's consider this disconnect argument from the perspective of history. Once upon a time, about 300 years ago, we effectively had no medicine, minimal technology, and limited intergroup communication/relations in most areas of the world. Ergo, humans had to *struggle* to survive using more primitive means like hunting, farming, basic trade, basic service procurement, and basic economics.

Living in a more primitive, or survival-oriented, world meant that our more reactive fear drive was quite useful. Essentially, because we had minimal technology and very small numbers with which to fight and survive, fear was a ubiquitous catalyst for both our cultural and personal stability. We needed to live a more reactionary lifestyle due to the great uncertainty of physical health issues (i.e., disease acquisition and management) and limited intergroup connectivity.

It stands to reason that if you don't know whether some new group of land inhabitants is peaceful, or whether this group carries life-threatening disease, being on the defensive (i.e., fearful speculation/proactive fearful aggression) makes sense. Somewhat unknowingly, this struggle for stability and general defensiveness also meant the advancement of the predominant individual/culture group with minimal dividends, if not major detriments, for the losers. I would propose that this process of dominant culture success is partly responsible for many of the "isms" and prejudices seen nowadays.

I propose that we take the above-mentioned example and compare it to the status of our medical, technological, intellectual, and social capacity today. In the realm of medicine, we have the knowledge and means to cure and eradicate bacterial infections that would have destroyed entire civilizations 300 years ago.

We have technology and medicine that can prevent, or at least ameliorate the symptoms of, most known diseases now. As a result, for instance, according to the World Health Organization (1) the average life expectancy the world over has increased by 5 years between 2000 and 2015 due to our advances in preventative medicine and sanitation practices.

Intellectually speaking, there have been amazing discoveries regarding our understanding of more complex phenomenon, starting with Newton's work on physics in the late 17th century up through the sequencing of the human genome in the late 20th century by Watson and Crick. We also have a more advanced understanding of simpler phenomenon like how plants grow, which has contributed manifestly to our ability to farm and develop agricultural businesses.

Socially, we can connect with anyone anywhere in the world thanks to cellular technology and the Internet. This almost instantaneous access to a person not in our immediate presence has drastically changed our expectations in many parts of the world about how quickly and in what manner we communicate and relate to each other, which I will discuss later as a potential mitigating factor for the problem of fear.

Also, the greater connectivity we have between and within societies has advanced our social and moral reasoning process. Three hundred years ago Western and Middle Eastern countries would have traded African natives as slaves or dictatorially usurped power in other countries around the world for both economic and socially immoral reasons. Whereas now—most people hope—we have respect for and a better understanding of other cultures and countries.

Most "civilized" countries now respect the sovereignty, dignity, and worth of African cultures. We understand they are not "lesser" or "inferior" groups that deserve, or "need to be," enslaved "for their betterment" and financial gain, despite these African cultures' different lifestyles compared to what you would see in Western countries. Power usurping...well that's an ongoing phenomenon; it just looks more diplomatic in some cases.

Thanks to evolution, we have achieved great advances in our moral, social, intellectual, and medical capacity due to our advanced neocortical development. So, why are we still operating like cavemen when it comes to world politics and many daily interpersonal exchanges? I propose that this brain-evolution disconnect described above is to blame.

Even though we can understand and critically think through millions of social and interpersonal situations, we do not choose to do so on a regular basis. Most people typically just "react" and do, as opposed to stopping and thinking through a situation fully. Something about how our emotional mid-brain is "wired" (or not) into our higher up reasoning and planning parts of the brain is keeping us stuck in caveman mode when it comes to phenomenon like affairs, greed, hatred, bigotry, and religiously motivated violence, which are only a handful of the millions of examples of this problem.

Even though humans had almost identical brain structures and proportions of white and grey matter 300 years ago, with a slight increase in white matter over the last 100 years (2), human societies have advanced intellectually, technologically, and culturally so much so that this primitive fear-based way of being is now counterproductive.

It would be facile to assert that because poverty is a problem and ISIS is attacking cultures around the world, we need to continue to get hijacked by our evolutionarily adaptive fear response in situations like not getting a text message from someone when you want to talk with them. I believe, however, that in most first world countries there is no need for a defensive, fear-based, orientation to everyday life and even major problems like terrorism.

Before diving into the biological bases of fear, it is important to note that there are multiple competing theories about and definitions of concepts like stress, fear, and anxiety. I've already differentiated the types of psychologically-distinct fear responses/process in the previous chapter: instinctual versus learned fear.

The bioevolutionary approach is somewhat more complicated. For instance, fear is generally regarded as both a cognitive (i.e., negative or worrisome thought) and an affective (i.e., biological/behavioral) process. Anxiety, however, can more simply be considered a brain/body condition of cortisol or adrenaline flow triggered by an outside stimulus (3).

Well-respected authors like Jak Panksepp (4, 5) have researched and discussed the various anxiety, panic, and fear brain systems at length. In fact, if you're so inclined, I highly recommend Panksepp and Biven's book *Archeology of the Mind: The Neuroevolutionary Origins of Human Emotions.* As a formal note to all readers, scholars and laypersons alike, I am intentionally lumping fear and anxiety into the same concept for two reasons.

First, many of the same brain areas, neurotransmitters, and hormones are involved in an overlapping manner for the various forms of semantically differentiated fear. Second, my goal is not to re-write an emotion/ evolution/brain textbook, because others have and can do it better than I. To sift through and explain the various forms of fear or anxiety definitions and research bases would be tedious and unproductive for our purposes.

Theoretically, at the very least, a low-level form of stress or anxiety about something we experience or believe will evolve into either a panic or pervasive fear issue if left to fester. I propose that, regardless of whether we label the subjective experience as fear or anxiety, very similar and related reactive and proactive behaviors emerge. Therefore, I define fear as a biologically-based (i.e., brain/body and neurochemical/hormone) feeling that is accompanied by typically negative or worrisome thoughts.

My goal at the end of the day is to give you an accurate and sufficiently detailed picture of the brain-body-mind experience of fear so you can understand what's happening to you when you haven't had 500,000 people like your Instagram post—discuss why we have fear, then identify and manage it better than our 18th century counterparts did.

This cognitive-affective experience of fear is the driving force in the examples of both positive and pathological behaviors I outlined in the introductory chapter. I propose, therefore, that our broadly defined experience of unchecked fear, considered as either strong anxiety or the more cognitive-affective "fear," is a major source of many individual, cultural, and global issues prevalent in today's world. Now I think it's important to explore our behavioral expression of fear, which will be the focus of my "consequences" sections later in the book, as well as how fear is being "driven" by common phenomenon in chapter 3.

Behavioral Manifestations of Fear

Until this point, when discussing fear, I've kept the focus on more obvious or reactionary versions of fear. There are, however, more subtle and long-term behavioral manifestations of fear. For instance, in the introductory chapter I described some behaviors as "proactive-aggressive" manifestations of our fear response.

The prototypical behavioral model in psychology for behaviorally managing fear is the "fight or flight" response (13), originally conceptualized in the 1930s and refined by modern psychologists to include freezing behaviors. This fight or flight phenomenon is considered our adaptive innate (i.e., hardwired) set of strategies—informed by neurochemistry and cortisol—for dealing with perceived threats.

This generally makes sense because threats, depending upon their seriousness and proximity, will demand different strategies. Some things we simply need to escape, so we engage in flight behaviors. Some circumstances are, unfortunately, not truly amenable to an escape strategy, so we must fight to de-escalate the threat. Our "freezing" behavioral strategies in the face of perceived threats might seem counterintuitive. The truth is, in the animal kingdom, some predators will lose interest in prey if they appear to be dead—the challenge is no longer there and the meat might be spoiled. Moving forward we will focus on the brain processes involved in fear, but rest assured we will double back to this introductory discussion of the behavioral manifestations of fear.

Fear in the Brain

When it comes to explaining our fear experience there are many useful paradigms in the psychology, evolutionary biology, and neuroscience literature. Given that this is a more applied book and not a graduate school textbook on neuroscience or psychology, I will attempt to give a simple overview of the basic biological and psychological components of fear in humans.

The hope here, in addition to educating you on the why and how of the basic fear processes you experience daily, is to provide you with a sense of *agency* in managing your affective states like fear. Knowledge is power, and I dare say we have felt powerless to our negative emotional states for millennia, which has resulted in much unnecessary suffering for millions of people.

Neurological and Chemical Bases of Fear

If you think back to the introductory chapter, I mentioned an example of how we can destroy certain parts of the brain and, essentially, operate without fear. Although this statement is an oversimplification of a complex instinctual neurobehavioral process, the truth is fear is expressed and modulated by a relatively small number of chemicals and brain areas.

Of the prevailing theories on fear, the most recent and comprehensive review comes from the work of Kindt (6) in Amsterdam. The predominant brain areas involved in our fear response include those responsible for sensation/perception (i.e., insular cortex, thalamus, and parts of the brainstem), memory (i.e., hippocampus and amygdala), and emotion/motivation (i.e., amygdala, periaqueductal grey, and ventromedial hypothalamus) (7, 8). This makes sense because if you think of any situation wherein we experience fear we usually need to perceive the threatening stimulus/situation, which causes a fear reaction, then remember things quickly that will help us determine how to act, and then have motivation (i.e., emotion) to survive/cope with the threat.

Of these brain areas related to the perception and meditation of our fear response, the one most authors discuss at length is the amygdala. It is responsible for fear memory, and it is particularly involved in our perception of seemingly threatening stimuli, even to the point where it can differentiate fearful facial expressions (10, 11).

The predominant chemicals involved in our fear response are norepinephrine (12), cholecystokinin, and cortisol. Norepinephrine and cholecystokinin are produced in the brain, and cortisol is produced by the adrenal glands on top of your kidneys. Cortisol, however, is secreted in response to perceived stressors, and it not only prepares your body to deal with anxiety, but it also enters into the brain and modifies activity in the anxiety and memory production areas of the brain mentioned above (13, 14). Another great book on cortisol and fear/stress is *Why Zebras Don't Have Ulcers* by Robert Sapolsky, which nicely details the destructive nature of excessive and/or prolonged exposure of humans to cortisol— our primary stress/fear hormone.

Essentially, all the chemicals work together in a symphony of activity throughout the brain and body to ready our senses, primal thinking, and bodily states to either run or stay and fight. Moreover, our brain is designed in such a way that when we experience even mild stress (i.e., cortisol) that we can even have more neutral stimuli activate a fight or flight experience (15).

On the flipside of the equation, the areas of the brain responsible for managing fear are the *medial prefrontal cortex* (i.e., MPFC) and parts of the *anterior cingulate cortex* (i.e., ACC). The predominant chemical in the brain responsible for anxiety amelioration is gamma aminobutyric acid (i.e., GABA). This GABA compound is the "chill out" chemical because it literally acts to slow down the activity of any neuron it attaches to in the brain.

GABA is the main brain chemical system activated by anti-anxiety drugs like benzodiazepines (e.g., Xanax or Klonopin) and addictive substances like marijuana and alcohol. Therefore, for the sake of oversimplification, our "frontal" (i.e., MPFC and ACC above your eyes) parts of the brain are responsible for tracking and dampening our midbrain sensory and emotional areas.

Relating back to that example in the introductory chapter where a part of the brain was destroyed that, essentially, eliminated fear in monkeys, the authors destroyed the amygdala, right? Unfortunately, loss of fear and fear learning is not the only consequence of destroying the amygdala, so that's not a reasonable approach to ameliorating the fear problem.

If we destroyed the part of our brain responsible for instinctual fear (i.e., necessary fear), then we would be putting ourselves in danger when we find ourselves in realistically threatening situations like fights, healthy competition, and other reasonable threats to our wellbeing (9). Now, this is an oversimplification of the fear process in terms of memory, behavioral expression, and visceral responses to threats, but the experimental research shows that we can, essentially, live without a strong conscious response to threats.

How Fear Happens

There is no simple way of separating out the psychological and chemical reactions based upon where these chemicals are active in the brain, so I will try to describe the process of being afraid from a neurochemical perspective using a relatable and relatively neutral example.

Think of yourself walking alone down a side street or an alley in a big city like New York, Chicago, or Los Angeles late at night, around 1 A.M. As you walk you hear footsteps behind you that seem to be getting closer.

You glance backwards and notice that there is a shadowy figure in a hooded sweatshirt following you, but you can't really discern who the person is, what the person looks like, or what they seem to be doing.

You speed up your pace to try and determine whether the person walking uncomfortably close behind you will speed up as well (i.e., is following you). You notice that the person keeps up with your pace. You begin to walk even faster and head towards a well-lit area near a busy gas station. The person's footsteps continue to match your own and get closer and closer to you as you near the busy gas station. Finally, you dash across the street to the gas station.

When you turn around, you see that the person behind you is gone, nowhere in sight. So…what happened in your brain and body? Well, the specifics would depend upon any previous experiences you've had walking alone at night in a big city; however, for our purposes just assume you're a typical non-traumatized or non-assault victim. Let's break this example down into a series of four "scenes" outlining behaviors, context, and brain activity.

Scene 1: Walking alone at night in an alley in a big city.

- Behavior: Walking.
- Context: Alone, late at night, in an alley, in a big city known for assaults.
- Brain:

  Sensation/perception areas: sense the alone and nighttime aspects.

  Frontal areas: process the context and any previous learning about the dangers of walking alone at night.

  Emotional/motivational areas: start sending signals to the frontal/motor parts of the brain to be alert and signal your adrenal glands on your kidneys to release a small dose of cortisol to "prepare" you.

Scene 2: Hearing footsteps behind you while walking alone.

- Behavior: Hearing footsteps behind you and speeding up your pace.

- Context: Alone, late at night, in an alley, in a big city known for assaults.

- Brain:

  Sensation/perception areas: hear the footsteps and feel your body tense up without thinking; begin communicating with frontal area.

  Memory areas: begin to recall real (i.e., personal experiences and news reports) and fictional (i.e., movies, shows, etc.) examples of people hurt or mugged while walking alone at night.

  Frontal areas: process the potential meanings of footsteps and any previous learning about the dangers of walking alone at night.

  Emotional/motivational areas: start sending signals to the frontal parts of the brain to increase your level of alertness, begin to release norepinephrine to motivational areas of the brain for readiness, and signal your adrenal glands on your kidneys to release a larger dose of cortisol to "prepare" you.

Scene 3: Footsteps speed up behind you and then seeing the gas station

- Behavior: Hearing footsteps behind you speeding up and seeing the gas station.

- Context: Alone, late at night, in an alley, in a big city known for assaults, beginning to see a safe area, seemingly increasing threat.

- Brain:

  Sensation/perception areas: hear the footsteps speed up; feeling your body tense up as a reaction to perceived threat; seeing the gas station; communicate with frontal and emotion/motivational areas.

  Memory areas: increased speed of recall of real (i.e., personal experiences and news reports) and fictional (i.e., movies, shows, etc.) examples of people hurt or mugged while walking alone at night; recalling reasonable strategies for dealing with perceived threat after seeing the gas station.

  Frontal areas: process the potential meanings of increased speed of footsteps; developing a plan to avoid perceived threat; incorporating use of gas station into plan for avoiding perceived threat.

  Emotional/motivational areas: increased rate sending signals to the frontal parts of the brain to increase your level of alertness; increased rate of release of norepinephrine to motivational areas of the brain for readiness; increased strength of signal to your adrenal glands on your kidneys to release an even larger dose of cortisol to help you have energy to escape.

Scene 4: You dash across the street, reach the gas station, turn around to find no one.

- Behavior: Running across the street, turning around, looking for the threat.

- Context: Well-lit area, around people, late at night, in a big city known for assaults, seemingly safe.

- Brain:

  Sensation/perception areas: feeling your body tense up and heart rate increase as you dash across the street; seeing no one behind you decreases sensory alertness; increase communication to frontal areas of the brain.

  Memory areas: decreased speed of recall of real (i.e., personal experiences and news reports) and fictional (i.e., movies, shows, etc.) examples of people hurt or mugged while walking alone at night; recalling reasonable strategies for dealing with perceived threat after seeing the gas station due to frontal area input.

  Frontal areas: process the level of threat resulting in a belief about being safe because you're around others in a well-lit area, as well as not being able to see anyone nearby who could have been following you; sends signals to memory and emotional/motivational areas to decrease alertness.

  Emotional/motivational areas: decreased rate of sending signals to the frontal parts of the brain to increase your level of alertness; decreased rate of release of norepinephrine to motivational areas of the brain for readiness; decreased strength of signal to your adrenal glands on your kidneys to slow release of cortisol which helped you have energy to get to the gas station. After approximately five to ten minutes, all hormone and neurochemical activity goes back to baseline.

So, that was a very brief and minimalistic explanation of how your brain, mind, and body all work together to evaluate, react, and act in a seemingly threatening situation. I want you all to notice a few things about the breakdown of the theoretical example.

First, of all the four scenes, no one scene can stand alone. All the reactions and brain processing occur in an overlapping sequence, and the context is key. The brain and body would react very differently if you turned around as soon as you heard the footsteps and saw a little old nun.

Second, no one brain area worked in isolation. Although some areas of the brain can act more independently, like your emotion/motivation areas automatically (without thinking/using frontal areas) causing your adrenal glands to release cortisol, rarely is one part of the brain acting alone to cause changes in behavior.

The brain areas discussed in the examination of this example were constantly communicating back and forth with each other, which is actually true regardless of threats—all of our brain areas are always communicating with each other. Finally, notice that it's not just your brain automatically reacting to a threatening situation. Like almost every experience we have there are contextual issues, hormones, emotions, biases, and expectations that affect how we act and react.

This symphony of chemicals, hormones, and brain processing is essentially no different across the various kinds of threats we commonly experience. Seeing a lion running towards you is going to elicit this fear response. Even the most menial threats, like not getting a text message back from someone you know or feeling threatened by a younger/more attractive/more accomplished person in a social situation, initiate this fear response process.

What varies among the brain/mind/body experiences during fearful situations are the length of time cortisol is flowing and the amount of emotional overwhelming that occurs to the point that our frontal cortex cannot process/manage our emotions. More intense or potentially extreme threats will more strongly overwhelm our frontal cortex's ability to manage what we're experiencing, which can be useful or not—depending upon whether we need to fight and be more primal.

Research has shown that a significant amount of fear (i.e., mediated by the amygdala, cortisol, and norepinephrine) can significantly cut off communication to our frontal lobe. If we're particularly hijacked, it is biologically impossible to think through things.

Summary

So, from the biological and psychological point of view we have highly developed frontal brain areas and reasoning capabilities that mediate or modulate our more emotional midbrain areas. Our frontal areas, communicating with our memory areas, account for the context of our situation, previous learning/information, and current skills/beliefs when trying to deal with something we experience that causes a strong emotional reaction.

Many of our emotional experiences cause automatic body and brain reactions (i.e., the stress hormone cortisol to release) that prompt us to react and behave in a more primitive manner. It is this battle, I assert, between our automatic emotional reactivity and our frontal/reasoning skills that is being lost daily. We have learned (i.e., learned fear) to treat many non-life-threatening experiences (e.g., social media bullying, political rhetoric, or even liking different sports teams) as life-threatening—eliciting our strong fear response.

Here's one final example, and it will be emotionally challenging so please bear with me. I believe we have this strong fear-based delusion in the U.S. wherein many individuals, media groups, and other politicians consider their opponents or opposite party individuals to be as threatening as a potential terrorist attack.

How many times in a day have you heard someone say that presidential candidate X would destroy the country or that their opponent was a horrible person? In the 2016 U.S. presidential election, people compared conservative presidential candidates to Hitler and liberal candidates to Stalin. Really? They're that destructive? Give me a break. Politicians and their policies in the U.S. can be harmful, but not like the Holocaust.

The fact of the matter is neither candidate would cause the country to collapse. They might make their citizens' way of life more challenging with a bad tax plan or some other policy. People could lose jobs or become marginalized, however, those instances are not the same as those that are life-threatening in most cases.

It would be tragic if your cultural group became or remained marginalized, and we should do something to help those who are suffering. Many of the laws already in place in most countries like the U.S. would be very difficult to repeal or dismantle to the point where people's civil rights disappear and millions die in one term of a presidency. No first-world country is perfect or treats all of its citizens well, but we have evolved too much for fully functioning societies to just collapse into World War II-era Machiavellian political change.

Also, as a reaction to our fear about leaders hurting us, we have developed this odd delusion of omnipotence about presidents. Presidents cannot wave a magic wand and end racism or solve economic issues. This is a point I will discuss further in chapter 5 when I fully discuss the implications of unchecked fear on cultures and societies.

I'm not advocating to just sit back and say nothing about your political beliefs or your worries about social issues. The real question I'm posing to you is this: do you need to get *that hijacked* about politics? Do you need to have that strong of a fear response about something that's out of your control (essentially)?

REFERENCES

1.   World Health Organization (2016). Monitoring the health goal: Indicators of overall progress. (Ch. 3). Retrieved on August 27th, 2016 from: http://www.who.int/gho/publications/world_health_statistics/2016/EN_WHS2016_Chapter3.pdf?ua=1

2.   Scientific American. (2013). How has the human brain evolved? Retrieved September 18, 2017 from: https://www.scientificamerican.com/article/how-has-human-brain-evolved/

3.   Steimer, T. (2002). The biology of fear- and anxiety-related behaviors. *Dialogues in Clinical Neuroscience, 4*(3), 231–249.

4.   Panksepp, J. (1998). *Affective Neuroscience: The Foundations of Human and Animal Emotions.* New York: Oxford University Press.

5.   Panksepp, J. & Biven, L. (2012). *Archaeology of Mind: The Neuroevolutionary Origins of Human Emotions.* New York: Norton.

6.   Kindt, M. (2014). A behavioural neuroscience perspective on the aetiology and treatment of anxiety disorders. *Behaviour Research and Therapy, 62*, 24-36.

7.   Shin, L. M., & Liberzon, I. (2010). The Neurocircuitry of Fear, Stress, and Anxiety Disorders. *Neuropsychopharmacology, 35*(1), 169–191. http://doi.org/10.1038/npp.2009.83

8.   Killcross, S., Robbins, T.W., & Everitt, B.J. (1997). Different types of fear-conditioned behavior mediated by separate nuclei within amygdala. *Nature, 388*, 377-380.

9.   Panksepp, J., Fuchs, T., & Iacobucci, P. (2011). The basic neuroscience of emotional experiences in mammals: The case of subcortical FEAR circuitry and implications for clinical anxiety. *Applied Animal Behaviour Science ,129*(1), 1-17.

10.   Adolphs, R. (2008). Fear, faces, and the human amygdala. *Current Opinion in Neurobiology, 18*(2), 166-172.

11.   Wang, S. et al. (2017). The human amygdala parametrically encodes the intensity of specific facial emotions and their categorical ambiguity. *Nature Communications, 8,* doi:10.1038/ncomms14821

12.   RIKEN (2017, September 18). Learning and Unlearning Fear: The Two Faces of Noradrenaline. *NeuroscienceNews.* Retrieved September 18, 2017 from http://neurosciencenews.com/nordrenaline-fear-learning-7512/

13.   Drexler, S.M., Merz, C.J., Hamacher-Dang T.C., Tegenthoff M., & Wolf, O.T. (2015). Effects of cortisol on reconsolidation of reactivated fear memories. *Neuropsychopharmacology, 40*(13), 3036-3043. doi: 10.1038/npp.2015.160.

14.   Bradford-Cannon, W. (1929). *Bodily changes in pain, hunger, fear, and rage.* New York: Appleton-Century-Crofts.

15.   Dunsmoor, J.E., Otto, A.R., & Phelps, E.A. (2017). Stress promotes generalization of older but not recent threat memories. PNAS, doi:10.1073/pnas.1704428114

"Religion is an illusion and it derives its strength from the fact that it falls in with our instinctual desires."

SIGMUND FREUD
New Introductory Lectures on Psychoanalysis

CHAPTER 3:
SOCIAL FACTORS AND UNCHECKED FEAR

Presuppositions

As you learned in the last chapter, our fear response is driven by a brain mechanism that can be triggered by either innately scary phenomena or situations, persons, places, or things that we have learned to fear. I've been proposing that our learned fears have gotten out of control, but have yet to discuss what specifically might be contributing to our fear problem.

It is no secret that the world is riddled with social and technological phenomena that contribute to what I propose to be our unchecked fear problem. You could go to any country in the world and handpick just one big umbrella phenomenon and spend years debating how it impacts the people in the region, that region's cultures, and world politics.

To keep this book from becoming hundreds of pages in length, I have decided to choose four of what I consider to be the most impactful phenomena in our fear driven societies. There are entire books devoted to each of these topics, so this will be more a cursory or superficial analysis. I hope, however, that my analysis is fair and accurate.

The goal of this chapter is twofold. First, I want to challenge you, in a fair and intellectually honest manner, to examine your relationships to these four phenomena and how you're involved in or swayed by the *hijacking* nature of said phenomena. Second, I want to provide a more psychologically nuanced viewpoint from which we can all understand why we react and then proceed forward in handling issues related to or arising from these four phenomena.

Once you discover the four phenomena I've chosen, you might become wary of my motives, so please do your best to judge my arguments and conclusions for their own merit. As a reminder, this is not some intellectualized atheistic or communist attack on any of your deeply held beliefs.

The goal for this section of the book is simply to try and objectively showcase the consequences of our fearful adherence to these four phenomena. The four phenomena that I believe contribute manifestly to our unchecked fear problem across most parts of the world are as follows: technology, politics, religion, and greed.

One final caveat. As a scholar, I try to own up to what I know and don't know, or at least know with some degree of certainty. Many of the arguments I will make are more subjective in nature but are supported by what I believe to be common sense and facts you can double check should you doubt what I propose.

I know my Western socialization and living in the United States is going to bias how I make arguments. I also wish to say that I am not sociologist, political expert, religious scholar, or economist and am not claiming any special expertise in said disciplines. I graciously submit my arguments discussed below to anyone of expertise or experience beyond my own, which I imagine to be many people, and would appreciate any feedback.

My hope is to simply begin illuminating important components of the global-social problem of unchecked fear. These four phenomena are salient issues across the world and they seem like the best avenues to wander down because of their widespread impact on almost every group of people.

Technology

When discussing technology there are two very prominent developments that I propose contribute to our unchecked fear problem: Social media and internet-ready smartphones. The Internet has been around for about 25 years and smartphones for roughly 20 years. For example, the first major social media site, Myspace, was created in 2003. These are historically very young phenomena, but they have become astoundingly prominent components of everyday life.

It is fair to say that these technological advancements are not innately bad or harmful—thinking back to the gun argument. I assert, however, that our relationship to these amazing technological developments has become hijacked by our evolutionarily necessary fear response.

The way we use this technology showcases what appears to be our now *almost desperate need* for connection and validation, even though social media and internet technology paradoxically allow us to get validation so easily and quickly. For better and for worse, these technological developments have become the vehicles for an almost instantaneous social feedback process, which has in turn modified our expectations about privacy and intimacy.

Let's use cyberbullying as an example of how technology can contribute to our fear hijacking problem. For the last 10 years or so there have been dozens of stories about cyberbullying and its tragic consequences when it's taken to the extreme (1). The most common examples of cyberbullying seem to be direct verbal harassment on social media or via text message, or, more notably, bands of people creating social media campaigns against other kids at school or work to demean them because they're ugly, gay, or not in the "in" group.

I doubt this is what Mark Zuckerberg intended to happen when he created Facebook. But why are millions of kids *and* adults engaging in cyberbullying on every kind of social media platform? Fear.

Fear of not being in the "in-group." Fear of being perceived as unpopular. Fear of not being accepted. If we associate with someone who is unpopular, unattractive, or part of a minority, then we're automatically in the "out" group.

Heaven forbid we simply judge people by the entirety of their character or personhood...but still, this is a common (statistically speaking) occurrence. There is a sad, yet understandable, reason as to why many people on social media engage in reactionary attacking and ostracizing of their peers: the out-group is "dangerous" to our way of being (i.e., defensive fear-based responding).

When we feel left out or ostracized, we have a natural strong negative emotional reaction because it means our genes might not survive. When we feel included and validated, we are happy and feel safe (2,7). I would say, however, that our very reasonable need to have peer validation has become hijacked by the expectations *we* have created about how to participate in and manage the rapid pace of modern technology like social media.

Imagine if it were 40 years ago. We would have to take a photograph with a film camera, wait to have it processed, then either show it to people in person, print it in a magazine, or mail it out to people. It would take at least a week for people to see what we're up to using pictures and judge our appearance.

Now, it's considered "weird" if we do not immediately receive likes, comments, and reposts of our social media. Moreover, to not participate in social media, or, if you're not trying to showcase how your lifestyle is great or commensurate with the standards of some "in" group then you're also considered weird.

Obviously, without social media and rapid communication technology like smartphones and tablets, we would not be able to really engage in cyberbullying. Platforms like Facebook, Twitter, Instagram, and Snapchat were created with the intention of maintaining connection with people and showcasing current events in our lives. These are healthy intentions because we all need to be "seen" and stay connected to be healthy and grounded (2).

However, as platforms like these became more profitable and more widely-utilized, various industrialized cultures and subcultures (e.g., business, fashion, music, performance, etc.) began exploiting these platforms. Nowadays, across many industries all over the globe, you must have a large social media following to be considered "legitimate" in your respective field.

Moreover, industrialized cultures that are more focused on body image—beyond what our evolutionary programming dictates for finding mates—push for being "hotter" or more renown than your friends. For example, if you search for the "most liked" photos on Instagram, it will most assuredly be of someone famous and very attractive (3, 4). How many provocative "at the gym" pictures, fancy meal pictures, and notable event pictures do you see daily on your social media?

So, let's look at this desire to be attractive and liked on social media more closely. Is it reasonable for everyone on social media to be perceived as "hot" or have the most fun and luxurious lifestyle? No, not at all. Most individuals live a more mundane life and are of average attractiveness—unlike celebrities and extremely wealthy individuals.

We have, therefore, become *obsessed* with living a life that's unreasonable or unattainable. When we fail to live up to these unreasonable standards, we feel ostracized, which exacerbates our extant self-esteem issues, which I will discuss in detail in the next chapter. A common question my fellow psychologists raise is: what reasonable influence should social media have on the average person?

If our evolutionary programming promotes "staying connected" and "being liked," then it would make sense to engage in some degree of social media participation. As society and technology evolve, so does our blueprint for connectivity and validation. Therefore, I propose that feeling an urge to participate is normal. But how strong should the "urge" to participate be? It's hard to say because, again, social media has become a statistically normal way of communicating and receiving validation.

I personally hope you all could be having a more detached relationship with your phone and your social media; however, it seems as if most people of all ages are now obsessed. Literally obsessed, as you might see it defined in the DSM-5, the diagnostic handbook for doctors and therapists (5).

If you took a straw poll of social media users, I would wager that many are at least slightly concerned about how many likes their photograph will garner or how many people see their post. Many people I know feel very strongly compelled to post attractive pictures or spin their latest dinner party as something "so fun!" If we consider this obsession, this hijacking of our normal desire to be seen and liked, from the perspective of the amount of time spent on social media, many studies average out to something like over four hours per day in industrialized countries (6).

That's four hours of superficial connection and staring at a screen, as opposed to face-to-face interaction wherein we truly feel connected, seen, and emotionally satisfied (7). Four hours of seeking validation online. Moreover, a recent survey showed that 78 percent of people in the U.S. had at least one social media profile (8).

In a world with constant connection due to population increases and rapid communication technology allowing for instant validation, do we really need to worry all that much about who is posting what and whether people like your post? No.

It's my belief that our natural need for connection, assisted by rapid communication technology and social media, has been hijacked by various cultures and subcultures. Our cultures have taken two amazing gifts and made them unnecessarily competitive and important means of gaining social validation, which has resulted in a general attitude of fear-based relations online and in-person.

Remember, social media usage is a widespread, ever-growing, and *lucrative* phenomenon. As we've come to spend more time and rely on these technological gifts, we've also given them more power over our emotional reactivity by assimilating them into our schema and schedule of "imperative" or "normal" ways of relating. Based upon my experiences and relationships with people participating on social media in both large and small cities in the U.S., I can safely say that many people have significant levels of a fear response about their posts and pictures, a worry about how people will receive them.

Is that necessary? If your picture on Instagram gets 20 likes, will you be irreparably ostracized? Not at all...but that's exactly the worry that results in widespread fear-driven relationships to our technology.

We need to learn to let go of our perceived need for constant positive validation and this falsely exaggerated importance of technology. This proposed move towards less social media reliance may not be good for technology and media companies' bottom lines, but it would be a good first step towards decreasing the incidence of problems like cyberbullying and low self-esteem that contribute to our unchecked fear problem.

We cannot change our expectations about how to relate to technology until we check our emotions. Try telling an Iraq war veteran their PTSD-induced flashbacks aren't really happening…you think they'll automatically calm down? Nope. We must manage the feelings first, which I will discuss at length in the last chapter.

Politics

One of the oldest social institutions in existence is politics. Although this is not a historical text, it is important to know when and where our problems started. Many academics consider ancient Greek democracy and ancient Roman republican politics to be the foundational forces for political thought in the industrialized world (9).

Even before the ancient Greek and Roman systems of political discourse in the 8th century B.C., there were likely more informal systems of governance in African tribal, Middle Eastern, South Asian, and Native American cultures. Hopefully anthropologists and other scientists will discover artifacts that explain the organization of the above-mentioned cultures and political systems.

Regardless of the theoretical influences of non-European cultures, the fact remains that informal political dealings have been a constant force since the beginning of organized civilizations. Every time one group of people has had power in a region there have been multiple outgroups competing for power.

If we fast-forward to 2017, political issues are some of the most incendiary and incessant topics discussed in countries all over the world. I am a citizen of the United States and we were in the midst of electing our next president when I was writing this text. I have had the displeasure of hearing from friends, family, news pundits, and colleagues alike absolutely disparaging and disheartening discourse about how the U.S. will collapse if their candidate does not win.

The intensity of the rhetoric and conjecture, with some facts sprinkled on top every once-in-a-while, feels so much more extreme than any other election I have seen. The vitriol of the 2016 U.S. election is worse than past elections I have heard about from those who are older (and much wiser) than I. For the purposes of keeping this brief, I will again focus more on the 2016 U.S. presidential election as an example rather than those in other countries because there are voluminous examples of politics causing social and physical harm to people readily available to you. Check out YouTube and you will find plenty of videos of politicians in many countries assaulting each other in their parliament houses and the like.

The standard question I ask in this chapter, and hope to answer effectively, is why a given phenomenon is such a problem. One factor that I believe plays a role in the hijacking of our fear response when it comes to politics is news media.

I simply cannot focus on the issues developing out of news media here because they deserve a full discussion in a separate book. Moreover, I believe that news media in the U.S. is such an insurmountable obstacle to emotional freedom. There are simply too many confounding and intractable variables in the news media problem, like money and power.

To simply illustrate the problem, I've included the following as a brief example of how the media contributes to the political problem in the U.S. If you do a quick search for news media discussions of how "nasty" or uncivilized the current presidential election has been, you will see numerous videos and stories by pundits and journalists describing how critical or "vicious" certain news stations or pundits have been in their discussion of a particular candidate.

It's noble that the media is pointing out how crude the discourse has become. The problem is...no one has stopped saying or propagating base or nasty speech. The media continues to hypocritically critique competing programs/pundits without cleaning up their own act.

Most major new organizations continue to run stories not based on facts, which are inflammatory and biasing. Making inflammatory statements is a great way to maintain viewership, promote a particular political ideology, and stir up the masses. So, I'd like to move on to more reasonable and resolvable issues in the U.S. political process and discourse. There are two topics in this section: bipartisan relations and our "culture of progress."

Bipartisan Relations

I believe the most prominent example of how politics plays a role in the hijacking of our fear response is the inherently bipartite nature of the U.S. political system. Yes, there are the ever-popular Independent, Libertarian, and Green parties, but our presidents almost always come from the big two: Democrats and Republicans.

It is true that George Washington, John Tyler, and Andrew Johnson were from non-major parties when they were elected president of the U.S. The fact remains though that modern U.S. politics has always been divided along the two-party, or as I think it would be better described, two-philosophy system.

Inherently, it would not necessarily be problematic to have a two-party system. The problem with a two-party system of political and social discourse is that the issues faced by U.S. culture are not simply remedied by having a totally conservative or liberal mindset.

Statistically speaking, if you look at polling data and voting record data, we can predict someone's beliefs about gun control based upon their beliefs about gay marriage. Conservatives typically vote one way on both issues and liberals typically vote in the inverse manner. I would assert, however, that the two issues are drastically different in terms of both their logistics and their implications.

A reasonable, rational belief about how to deal with guns is in no way similar to the issues (i.e., social, moral, religious) associated with gay marriage. A well-reasoned individual would likely borrow ideological positions from both major parties to make the healthiest and most reasonable choice for either issue.

This is, again, a problem of how we have defined ourselves by our political parties and given that meaning unnecessary power over our cognitive and emotional faculties, which is beginning to find support in neuroscience research (10).

Thinking back to the cyberbullying example in the previous section, it seems like we have allowed ourselves to develop a learned fear response to those people described as the "out group"—whomever does not align with your party of choice.

Is the fact that you vote democrat or republican really a core and essential aspect of your identity? I hope not, because we are more than our job, our political identity, or our sexual orientation. I believe all people would be healthier if they could understand the beautifully challenging and complex variables (hundreds of them) that make up a person. We need an integrated and balanced self-identity.

This two-philosophy political system and the way U.S. culture has decided to integrate it into personal identity has resulted in a problem psychologists call "black and white" thinking (11). When we're hijacked by our emotions, we tend to revert to more primitive ways of being and operating.

When our brains were young, before the age of two, we processed more in a black and white manner, all or nothing. We generally experienced things as promoting safety or danger. As our frontal cortex grew and we began to learn social/moral reasoning, we learned to see the shades of grey in experiences. I propose that the incessant two-party glorification in the U.S. by politicians, media, and everyday people promotes this primitive reactionary style.

Republicans are associated with all sorts of bad policies, figures, and close-mindedness. Democrats are likewise associated with morally reprehensible figures, dangerously liberal beliefs, and typically short-sighted fiscal policies. If you align with a third party, you're typically looked upon as a weirdo, akin to the people who don't participate in social media.

Political party (philosophy) choice in the U.S. is an instantaneous fear hijacker, and here are some simple examples to prove the point. First, I ask: how many times have you had a heated "discussion" with a friend, family member, or coworker about their liking of an opposing candidate? If *anyone* reading has never had an argument about politics, please contact me right away so I can learn your secret!

The reality of the situation is, if you're alive in the U.S. and are over the age of 18, you likely have engaged in arguments about politics at least a half dozen times in 2016 because the U.S. was in an election year. Imagine if you got rid of the two candidates in the 2016 U.S. election and tried to simply discuss the issues or problems of the country. This seems like a noble idea, right?

I can guarantee that at some point you or your "opponent" will blame the problem on "conservatives," "liberals," "republicans," or "democrats" and the conversation will quickly disintegrate into angry comebacks. But is it really a person's ideological group that is to blame for problems in making change?

No, because people can act reasonably regardless of party affiliation. They simply choose not to act in a more reasonable manner out of fear. Here's a final thought experiment to drive the point home.

Imagine for a moment you travel to a state in the U.S. where you do not live. You walk into a coffee shop and begin talking about the candidate of your liking with another patron who likes the opposing candidate. The chances are good that as soon as you hear in the conversation that this random stranger is for "the other side" your blood pressure will begin to rise (i.e., pre-emptive fear response making you more alert) and you will automatically from that point on have an attitude of circumspection about that person. Maybe I'm wrong. Maybe you would handle this theoretical situation with complete Zen or mindfulness—though I doubt it.

Why do we get angry at each other? Why do we automatically become wary of complete strangers when all they have said is "I think I like Donald Trump" or "I think Hillary Clinton is the better of two bad choices?" Fear.

Fear that the opposing person is going to win or that the opposite party candidate will irreparably damage your way of life. It is absolutely true that the President of the United States has great power. The President can influence our country and the world in both word and deed. I would propose, therefore, that it is reasonable to have a fear response when talking with someone if you distrust their candidate choice.

Fear is, again, a healthy response to perceived threats—past, present, or future. The more important question is: Do we really need to become so hijacked by our fear that we lash out in anger at each other and treat each other with contempt about politics? Does it really help us solve problems and move the country forward?

I've discussed this question with about ten of my psychologist friends and dozens of acquaintances across the spectrum of professions all over the U.S. The net result of almost all 60 or so conversations was a statement like this:

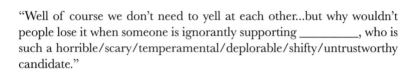

"Well of course we don't need to yell at each other...but why wouldn't people lose it when someone is ignorantly supporting _____, who is such a horrible/scary/temperamental/deplorable/shifty/untrustworthy candidate."

Their answers always included some statement about how reasonable it would be to get hijacked because people are afraid of something bad happening on Election Day—almost as if the world were going to come to an end. As a citizen of this democratic-republic kind of country, it would seem obvious to be invested in the choice of your next leader.

I would also say that it's more than reasonable to have some trepidation about candidates for president who appear dubious, radical, or ignorant. The question then becomes: Do I need to lose my cool during the election process? No. We've let our fear get the best of us.

The more we yell at each other and shoot passive-aggressive barbs back and forth across the table/bar the greater the divide becomes between us and reinforces our need to be afraid of those voting for the opposite party. This process of losing it on each other halts any ability to have a reasonable discussion of issues and arrive at a point of consilience.

There is also a plethora of secondary or sub-issues within the bipartisan problem like greed, special interest groups, foreign relations, religion, and general ignorance. I will, however, not be exploring those issues because many authors of note have discussed them at length.

Moreover, if I were to discuss those subtopics, my personal biases and beliefs would become a factor and distract you from the truly important objective arguments I hope I am making. I do not wish to throw my bias into the ring because the psychology of fear, examined objectively, as it relates to our relationship to politics is the real focus of this section.

A second major topic that is important to discuss without political bias is how our culture has become obsessed with making progress driven by governmental influence.

Culture of Progress

At first glance this sub-section title may seem like an attack on liberal or Democratic Party views, but it's not. This is not a critique of either dominant political philosophy. I am, however, making the statement that U.S. political culture has become unhealthily obsessed with either making or resisting progress.

Take, for example, the last 20 years of news coverage about the U.S. Congress. Almost like clockwork, when congress has been in session, there have been multiple stories about how "nothing was accomplished today" because some group of senators filibustered, or congressmen couldn't agree on a compromise regarding some law, budget, or issue.

Isn't that absolutely astounding? In a country like the U.S., this phenomenon is baffling to me. The people of the U.S. have a history of rebelling against intransigent political systems like autocracies and monarchies, fighting for civil rights, and developing a more reasonable and "free" way of being. Yet, now, we have tied our own hands with our inherent bias towards "keeping it the way we like it" or "making it better than it is." My essential argument is that our political system, driven by our national and individual fear problem, has been hijacked by a culture of progress and concomitant counter cultures.

Let's examine this progress phenomenon more closely. You might be thinking to yourself, "Well, why is progress bad?" I'm not arguing that a desire for progress is inherently bad. Change is a necessity for any culture, or individual, to survive and thrive. It is more than reasonable to want a "better" life.

The question that always comes to mind when I hear people crying out for "progress" or "change" driven by the political establishment is: What is the actual state of progress/change in the U.S.? It's important to know whether the situation is really as "bad" as it sounds.

Often social and political problems are examined by the media, or by ourselves, using only one narrow-minded perspective...which can make the problem seem worse than it might be. Perhaps, the situation is still not ideal, but much better than it has been in the past.

The second question I would then raise is: What is the rate of progress/ change compared to the rest of the world? One problem I believe many individuals and organizations in the U.S. struggle with is an ethnocentric or Eurocentric view of cultural progress.

If the litmus test for progress is simply the current state of affairs here in the U.S. or very progressive countries in Europe, then I think we truly don't know how bad the state of progress truly is. Issues like cultural discrimination, poverty, and healthcare are common "progress" topics discussed by both dominant political philosophies.

So, let's focus on one of these common progress topics and try to examine just how "bad" the state of progress is in the U.S. Again, please try to judge my arguments for their soundness and clarity, and not simply based upon your gut reaction to them. Your personal experiences of discrimination, like my own, do not factor into the veracity of the arguments or the existence of facts.

Prejudice and Progress for LGBTQIA Individuals

The umbrella topic of discrimination here in the U.S. is often taken up by both major political philosophies, sometimes agreeing on sub-issues but typically disagreeing. Again, I'm not here to pick a side. This is simply an example of how organizations and individuals on both sides of the political spectrum, aided by the media, capitalize on people's emotionality using conjecture and Machiavellian spins on facts to either push for change or keep the status quo.

When it comes to discrimination, the three biggest groups that typically are discussed in the U.S. are: ethnic/racial minorities, LGBTQIA individuals, and women. Many of you, like myself, belong to one or more of these groups and might have had a negative or discriminatory experience. This evaluation is simply a factual exploration of the problem, not an argument against any of your or my own lived experiences.

For the sake of simplicity, let's pick just one group and talk about "how bad" it is for said group simply based upon the facts. I would like to focus on the challenges faced by the LGBTQIA population in the U.S. As we explore the problems and the facts, try to notice the relative scoresheet of facts showing improvement for our queer friends versus the existence of problematic or regressive phenomenon. Then, I will discuss the overall rate of progress and assess how "bad" it really is for people in the LGBTQIA community—my interpretation of the facts.

I propose that we evaluate the problems faced by the LGBTQIA community in the U.S. from the perspective of three commonly-accepted social justice research domains (12): *basic human needs* (i.e., shelter, basic safety, sanitation, & finances), *opportunity* (e.g., legal change, research on acceptability, financial success, perceived discrimination), and essential components of *well-being* (i.e., perceived wellness, basic health, access to information/resources).

Regarding *basic human needs*, individuals in the LGBTQIA community typically do not struggle with maintaining nutrition, sanitation, money, or shelter; however, a significant proportion of homeless youth identify as somewhere on the queer spectrum (13). This implies that a significant number of queer-identified youth are either choosing to leave their houses due to actual or perceived prejudice/discrimination from family/community or that they are kicked out of their houses for many reasons. Already, you can see that while some basic aspects of the LGBTQIA experience are on the positive side, some are not.

Regarding *opportunity*, there are many complex issues. For instance, when it comes to advocacy and legal issues, the LGBTQIA community has had some success in the past decade in the U.S. with the striking down of DADT (14) and nationally legalizing gay marriage (15). There are also very clear anti-discrimination laws in place regarding the hiring and firing of individuals solely due to sexual identity (16), although not all states in the union have their own laws.

Unfortunately, the U.S. Equal Employment Opportunity Commission (EEOC) found that there was a 28 percent increase in the number of allegations of wrongful firing based upon sexual identity in 2015 (16); however, only approximately 48 percent of the cases were deemed fitting for remediation (i.e., justified). A study from 2013 found, essentially, no discrimination in four major U.S. cities when it comes to hiring LGBTQIA individuals (17). Another study found that 15 percent of LGBTQIA individuals experienced workplace discrimination based upon sexuality (18).

So, let's take a quick pause and evaluate just this one set of facts I've presented to you regarding LGBTQIA employment discrimination. On the one hand, there was an increase in the number of allegations. Many people would stick with that one fact alone and make catastrophizing statements. Then, we must evaluate the rest of the facts. Less than half of the cases were legitimate.

If you were to look at the EEOC website, listed in the references, you would find that more cases were resolved compared to last year and more people were rightfully compensated for their experiences of discrimination. In summary, on the one hand it is a problem that people are still being wrongfully fired; however, the number of LGBTQIA people wrongfully fired is decreasing and more LGBTQIA individuals are both advocating for themselves (i.e., they feel safe enough to stand up for themselves) and are being adequately compensated for their experiences of discrimination.

Mixed bag, right? The point is, some issues still exist. Prejudice exists. But it all depends upon looking at all the facts and comparing the trends.

Regarding the final category, wellness, there are many ways to evaluate the progress and continued problems in the LGBTQIA community. Perceived social support is one way of looking at wellness.

One study found that most gay and bisexual individuals felt supported despite perceived discrimination socially or experientially (19). Another study focusing on African American homosexuals found that 63 percent experienced some form of discrimination, but that close to 90 percent felt included in their community (20).

Another study found that smoking among female queer-identified youth was higher than same-aged heterosexual female youth, but queer identified female youth engaged and actively participating in gay-friendly communities were less likely to smoke (21).

An LGBTQIA survey group found that approximately 75 percent of queer-identified youth felt accepted by their peers, and 77 percent believed things will continually get better for the gay community (22). That same study, however, showed that queer-identified youth are twice as likely to be bullied or assaulted compared to heterosexual peers, and 42 percent said they did not feel accepted by the community at large.

An article in the *Huffington Post* a few years ago cited an advocacy group's finding that approximately 14 people were murdered purportedly due to their LGBTQIA identity (23). In my opinion, it is likely that the number of hate crime-motivated murders were underreported, in my opinion, it is and it was difficult to find reliable data on this topic.

So, the above sections are a representative snapshot of how far LGBTQIA individuals have come and what the struggle still looks like. I admit that the facts and figures I cited above are by no means exhaustive or perfectly representative of all the important statistics. I think it would be a reasonable or fair statement to make that the numbers have gone up for positive statistics, like perceived acceptance, and down for negative statistics, like number of wrongful firings or hate crimes.

Now, how about the rate of progress here in the U.S.? Based upon the facts above, it would be wise to compare how well LGBTQIA individuals are doing here relative to other marginalized groups in the U.S., not that the issues, biases, or barriers are in any way the same. It is also necessary to see how quickly things are changing and how "good" the state of affairs is here for LGBTQIA individuals compared to other nations.

Progress Rate Comparison in the U.S.

To compare the rate of progress here in the U.S., we can perform many logical maneuvers. For instance, we could compare the number of legal or social victories for the LGBTQIA population since the country's inception, and simply see how far things have advanced in the last 240 or so years. Then we could break it down more finely by topic or by year. Or, we could look at the number of hate crimes in the last year compared to the previous decade.

If we look at LGBTQIA legal progress since this country's inception, the most obvious statement one could make is that queer-identified individuals had no protections in 1776. Now, as of 2016, gay marriage is legal, antidiscrimination laws are in place for many sectors of society (i.e., education, employment, finances, etc.), and roughly 30 states have sexual orientation and gender hate crime laws. Broadly speaking, it would be fair to assert that the country has made significant progress in its relatively short lifespan, with most of the progress occurring in the last 30 years since the passage of the hate crimes statistics act in 1990 under George Bush Sr. (not so conservative, eh?).

Essentially, for around 200 years LGBTQIA individuals have had minimal to no equal or special legal protection in the U.S. Unfortunately, I could not find any hard numbers on how many LGBTQIA individuals have been denied employment, financial support, wrongfully fired, assaulted, or murdered since 1776, or even since the 1990s when LGBTQIA advocacy was beginning to explode in this country.

I cannot in good conscience describe any kind of progression or regression for LGBTQIA wellbeing simply given the lack of data. Economically speaking, it's difficult to discern relative privilege or hardship given the number of "closeted" individuals in the workforce. One older study, however, showed that gay men typically earn 32 percent less as compared to their heterosexual male peers and that roughly 64 percent of trans-identified individuals earn roughly $25,000 a year (29), well below the poverty line.

Given the lack of historical data on LGBTQIA incomes and economic opportunity, I again cannot make a statement about whether our queer-identified peers have made progress economically. Obviously, it's bad that the number of trans-identified individuals are in poverty, but hopefully that represents a decrease compared to 50 years ago. Until we have more data, the numbers simply represent current assessments, not trajectories of change. The trend in the data is more important for making a judgment about how to move forward with policy changes and fearful responses.

The basic LGBTQIA historical outline in the U.S. is this: more people are "out," more people are engaging in advocacy, more people are being treated with respect, and more people have more rights. Generally, it seems like gay rights in every sector are on an upward trend.

Rate of Progress Around the World

The next step is to compare the rate of LGBTQIA progress in the U.S. against the rest of the world. This comparison, however, might be more difficult because many countries are so varied in their cultural, geographic, legal, religious, and economic profiles that many circumstantial factors will speed up or slow their rate of progress.

If we take the amount of progress the U.S. has made in its very brief (240 year) history, in the context of when the U.S. was formed, how knowledge has spread, and societies have advanced in that time, and then compare it to other countries who are older/younger, more or less economically stable, religiously-run versus secularly-oriented, and more or less dense in terms of population, this evaluation process can get very messy.

As we've seen, the U.S. has made many advances in legal protections and freedoms for LGBTQIA individuals as we've already discussed. According to results published by the Human Rights Campaign (7), it seems as if many cultures are more rapidly pushing for LGBTQIA rights.

As of the beginning of 2016, over 19 countries had full marriage equality for LGBTQIA individuals, and Chile, Cypress, and Greece passed civil union laws. Now, that only represents 11 percent of the countries in the world with major world powers like Russia and China missing from the pro-gay rights movement. Moreover, multiple Southeast Asian countries like Thailand and Vietnam have passed equal protection for trans-identified individuals.

According to the statistics from the World Economic Forum, LGBTQIA individuals/companies bring in about three trillion dollars annually. Another interesting finding is that over two-thirds of Fortune 500 companies have anti-discrimination policies in place. Many of these advances in worldwide LGBTQIA progress have been initiated in the last 30 years.

Essentially, all the advancements for our queer-identified fellow man that countries have made have only happened recently. If we examine just these few facts, it seems like the U.S. is at the least on par with, if not ahead of, many countries that are much older and have been established and functioning in a "civilized" manner for much longer than the U.S.

The main premise of this chapter is how much fear we need to have and let inform our behavior. In this particular section, I've been discussing the problem of politically-driven pushes for progress and the resulting counter cultures. Looking at just one major group striving for politically and socially driven progress, the LGBTQIA culture, it seems as if there are still many problems and prejudices that require advocacy and political change. On the other hand, looking at the facts, it seems like queer-identified people in the U.S. have it good compared to many other parts of the world.

The U.S. does not appear to be falling behind or regressing, but is actually progressing at a reasonable or comparable rate. I would, therefore, propose that for those of us concerned about LGBTQIA progress there is much work to be done, but we do not need to maintain the alarmist attitude that many citizens continue to hold onto.

Living in a fear-based attitude only makes us feel worse and typically promotes progressive rights fighters to take action that alienates people on the other side of the argument, which in turn causes a surge in anti-progress movements. So, what's the solution? I believe we need mindful advocacy and healthy discussion between ideological opponents, which I will discuss in greater detail in a later chapter.

Religion

The third factor that seems to play a large role in the divisiveness and fear-based living of billions of people the world over is religion. Again, I want to remind you this is not a diatribe against religion—I am not attempting to convince you God doesn't exist or to give up your beliefs.

My hope is to show you how your reactions to the world around you, mediated by your religious beliefs, might be on the unnecessarily fearful side of the spectrum. Please, keep your religion and religious beliefs because I'm sure they're very helpful for you in many ways. I'm simply asking you to read on and ask yourself if you might be overreacting because of some of the stories and concepts you learned from your religious tradition.

Religion is a uniquely human phenomenon. Though some may believe there is a wide variety of religious differences, many religions share similar concepts or beliefs at their cores. There are anywhere between 200 and 4,300 various religions or subtypes of major religions.

Christianity purportedly has the most followers (approximately 2 billion) and Islam has the second most followers (approximately 1.5 billion), according to various polls and sources. Of the roughly 7 billion people on the planet, approximately half belong to only two religious groups. I want to add one caveat before I delve into my main arguments.

Religion and spirituality are very different concepts. While they may seem like similar concepts, if you look at their literal roots, you will see some interesting fundamentals emerge. Look at spirituality as it's derived from a literal belief in spirits or in spiritual beings. There actually is no substantive proof either for or against a belief in spirits. Although recently there have been a few evolving conversations among physicists and other scholars about the quantum nature of particles and how spirits or different kinds of consciousness may be related to our quantum nature (24, 25).

What's important to keep in mind, however, is that these arguments between physicists and other scholars are purely theoretical. No physicist or sane scholar is making statements like "get more spiritual" or "people who don't believe in spirits are in peril" or "kill non-believers" simply because it might be a possibility that spirits exist. It is, therefore, not wise to blame people's beliefs in spirits and spirituality simply because we do not know what exists.

No one is claiming to know anything with any real certainty. Plus, when is the last time you heard of someone randomly murdering someone else because they believe spirits exist? I doubt your yoga teacher is out mass-murdering anyone in the name of the "divine essence." For a better understanding of what spirituality "is" from a scientific perspective, I would read books like *Waking Up* by Sam Harris. My goal here is not to argue the plethora of definitions and validity of ideas, just to note that the two concepts are different pragmatically speaking, with different consequences typically.

Religion, on the other hand, is a readily-observable social construct that organizes people based upon their beliefs and rituals *about* spirits or god(s). Religion is a set of firmly-held guiding principles, broadcast throughout a group of like-minded individuals, about how to live based upon one's notions of spirits or god(s). Every religion has their own set of guiding principles that people use to develop their sense of morality, which informs the way they behave.

Orthodox Jews have their 213 laws. Islam contains dozens of laws about diet, sanitation, worship, money, work, and other areas of life found in their holy books, the Quran and Hadith. Christianity has the Ten Commandments, dozens of verses in the book of Proverbs, and over 1,050 commandmentss in the New Testament attributed to the apostles, God, and Jesus Christ. Buddhism has the eightfold path. Hinduism is slightly more ambiguous and subjectivist in its approach for prescribing a way of life based upon the dynamics of your Karma and Dharma. Jainism has approximately 35 rules of conduct.

Essentially, depending upon which religious system you choose, you are either encouraged or mandated to live a very different lifestyle. And here lies the problem with religion, not a particular religion—though some religion's believers have created more negative consequences than others.

The problem with religion is twofold, and all because *people* choose to act in irrational (i.e., fear-driven) ways based upon their religious beliefs. There is the problem of grouping in religion and then the problem of irrational validity. As we have already seen in the discussion of politics, when people begin grouping themselves based upon beliefs, then the most natural consequence of self-grouping is that out-groups are created and conflicts ensue.

There is a great quote from the movie *Men in Black* where one agent played by Tommy Lee Jones states, "A person is smart, people are dumb, panicky, dangerous animals and you know it." The question asked by Will Smith's character prompting this response was why the government didn't let the public know that aliens existed. The character played by Tommy Lee Jones was implying, rather poignantly, that herd mentality kicks in when we group up and are presented with threats (26).

Like it or not, we are still animals in many ways. When people believe their religious ways of being are being attacked by an out-group, then it naturally causes people to react in fear and live defensively, or proactively seek out and destroy those who theoretically threaten or oppose them.

All religions—just like philosophies—struggle with a problem of rationality (i.e., credibility) and validity. The argument I'm making here is similar to the credibility arguments that Bertrand Russell proposed about religion in the early 1900s (27).

Essentially, there are such widely varying and contradictory religious beliefs and practices across and within religions, which are supported by minimal or no substantive scientific proof for why those beliefs are "best." Often enough, these varying religious beliefs have resulted in countless deaths, prejudice, and cultural divisiveness. It then makes sense, based upon the premises of the grouping problem, that there are people wary of a particular religion (i.e., the out-group) or wary of religion in general (i.e., the meta-out-group, Atheists).

Unfortunately, many participants in a religious belief system have not engaged in any kind of intensive study about the true origins of their belief system and are not quite fully aware of the full historical and political context that drove the development of their religion. Without a full understanding of something, we tend to have very surface or superficial beliefs. Superficial beliefs are often easily challenged and highly inflammatory.

In terms of credibility, it is worth noting that most religions were created in a period before advanced scientific understanding of events like disease, earthquakes, weather, and other natural phenomena. Creating a belief system, or even a way of life, based upon a minimal understanding of how things work and fear-based cultural norms does not actually promote the most mindful, inclusive, or critically thought-through way of living. Knowing what you know about how things work now, why does it make sense to base your behavior on belief systems created in the Bronze Age?

For example, slavery was once widely accepted and *is* highly promoted in most Abrahamic religious texts. However, through socially- and scientifically-informed moral reasoning, we now have decided that slavery is wrong. Moreover, in most societies we also no longer believe we should kill people for disobedience of parents, infidelity, or homosexuality—though it still happens.

Now, the arguments I just made about the irrationality of religiously-driven behavior are both broad and seemingly inflammatory. I hope, however, that you see my point and can understand that my goal is to show the discrepancy in our individual thinking.

Many of us who appreciate and value religious beliefs do not hold to some of the more arcane moral imperatives of the Abrahamic texts because our moral reasoning is much more advanced now that we have all had some time to talk about and reflect on these various religious precepts. I think it would be fair to say that most Christians, Jews, and Muslims are not out killing children for misbehavior because they do not see the murder of disobedient children as a credible or reasonable moral behavior.

I also want to point out that there are many moral and virtuous components to all religions. Jainist, Hindu, Buddhist, Christian, Jewish, and Islamic texts all contain very pragmatic and moral philosophies. The problem is that amidst those moral commands, there are those immoral behaviors advocated purportedly "by God," that a subset of the religious world does not let go of in most religions—except for Jainism and Buddhism.

The human interpretation of religious texts that, at one time, advocated for what we now consider destructive behavior is a problem. Because we are human, we all have illogical fears and prejudices. Some passage in a holy book advocating murder or marginalization might open a door for acting out our illogical fears or prejudices with disastrous consequences.

ISIS is a perfect example of this phenomenon. Because of the many prescriptions for violence in the Quran and the Hadith, specifically about Jihad and spreading the faith to the rest of the world, extremist groups like ISIS are more likely to form in the name of the Islamic faith. On the other side of the spectrum, you don't hear of Jains going out and bombing each other or non-believers *because* nowhere in Jainist texts do you find prescriptions for violence—quite the opposite. I'll admit this is an oversimplification of a complex global phenomenon like ISIS and how it developed due to geopolitical and historical forces, but the basic reasoning is correct.

If our version of god advocates for some behavior people in the out-group consider immoral, it stands to reason that we feel less obliged to mindfully check our motives or care about the true magnitude of the consequences resulting out of our behavior.

When you combine the grouping problem—causing counter cultures and wars of ideas—with the lack of credibility problem, a fear-based dynamic develops. Even very reasonable religious people, who don't hate their ideological opponents, are prone to closing their minds when their beliefs are challenged.

Many religious people tend to dig in their heels and say, "Because God created my belief system, it cannot be wrong." This makes sense because the biggest religions tend to believe a lack of faith will send you to Hell—sounds very scary. This process of religion self-sustaining and rationalizing its validity with cyclical arguments, due to fear, is a problem. No one likes it when their beliefs are questioned, but this should not be a reason to become recalcitrant and aggressive.

This proactive-aggressive defensiveness (i.e., closed-mindedness) seen in religious reactors when challenged, combined with the grouping phenomena, means easy conflict all over the world. This is the problem with our fear-driven adherence to religions and religious principles; it induces closed-mindedness, which ultimately results in conflict.

Interestingly, some research is now demonstrating that people with damaged frontal areas of the brain (similar to how fear short-circuits our frontal lobe) actually become more zealous about their religion (30). This showcases the infinite loop problem I'm discussing: fear about religious belief-based judgment leads to less critical thinking because fear overwhelms our frontal cortex's abilities. This leads to an instinctual (i.e., tribalistic) response that, in turn, leads to more fear and aggression.

While this section addressed the problem with religion, I want to restate that this is not a refutation of religion. I made some statements that do provide a basis for refuting religion; however, the goal is to show the ideological or philosophical issues in practicing the most commonly adhered-to religions that typically result in conflict among both believers and non-believers, and how that creates an intractable fear-driven conflict loop.

What I am discussing is our very normal and human fear response to having an unusually certain understanding of things when most of us are confused about the why of life, the inconsistency of beliefs about our existential experience that results from being told to "live on faith," and having our beliefs constantly challenged. The problem is simply fear.

Fear that our reliance on faith or religion is wrong. Fear that our religion will be taken away. Reactive aggressive fear because God(s) want(s) us to do or believe in things the world at large disagrees with and criticizes on a regular basis.

Imagine simply having faith-based beliefs or religious beliefs and not feeling like you must defend or spread them? What would that require? Well, I'll discuss this more in my "solutions" chapter at the end of this book. Generally, what would be of the utmost value for ending this religion-driven fear problem is humbly acknowledging the limits of what we know and emphasizing that we are all human and deserve basic human respect and care—regardless of our religious beliefs. This is typically a tall order.

Greed

One of the more fundamental problems discussed the world over is money, and specifically greed. Indeed, one recent theory of civil war development (i.e., intra-country conflict) highlights how economic disparity born out of greed should be considered a primary driving force (31).

There are over 100 songs about wealth and money, thousands of investment firms, dozens of government agencies, schools of academic study devoted entirely to the art and science of making money, and countless other industries focused purely on helping people make money.

There's this great song from the musical *Cabaret* titled "Money Makes the World Go 'Round." Within the lyrics of this song are some ironically deep philosophical truths about how most people on this planet see and deal with money. The lyrics state that money helps us have fun, deal with relationship loss, escape problems, and ultimately allows us to eat and have warmth.

It seems to be particularly accurate when songs or literature assert that money is equated to a panacea for life's problems. So how does the seemingly reasonable utility of money that we all understand metamorphose into greed in many Western countries as well as the major Eastern world powers?

Well, before we delve into the fear-driven process of greed development and how it's commonly occurring in countries like the U.S., I think a clear definition of greed is important. There are numerous connotations that immediately arise in the mind when we hear the word greed. Maybe we think of unfairness or selfishness. Or, greed can elicit the image of an egomaniacal or money-grubbing individual.

The Oxford Dictionary (32) defines greed as the "intense and selfish desire for something, especially wealth, power, or food." I find this definition to be interesting because it specifies criteria of intensity and selfishness in terms of the intention/manner of acquisition of money, and not simply just having amassed wealth.

It would stand to reason that someone who makes billions of dollars only to give a large portion of it away would not be characterized as "selfish" or greedy. Or, on the other hand, someone who slowly and mindfully accumulates a large amount of money would also not be considered greedy because it doesn't meet the qualifier of "intensity."

Given this definition and understanding of greed, it seems reasonable to discuss the consequences commonly associated with greed-driven behavior; however, that will be saved for the next few chapters on the individual and cultural consequences of fear.

One more caveat. The purpose of this subsection discussing fear gone awry, as evidenced by more and more people acting in a greedy manner, is not to advocate for a communist model of economics. I'm neither arguing for or against any economic system.

There are dozens of scholars who have written about economics that can argue about this more fluently and accurately, and I have no desire to misrepresent my knowledge. I hope to provide a psychological and evolutionary perspective on why a certain percent of the population is engaged in greedy behavior or is driven by greed.

So how does greed develop? Again, the simple answer is evolutionary needs gone awry. The complex version about how our evolutionary need to survive and thrive is slightly lengthier.

The formula goes like this:

(misperceived) necessity + opportunity + fear = greed

Regarding necessity, when it comes to survival in the last, let's say, 4,000 years, we typically have needed to engage in hunting or bartering behavior to survive. Bartering resulted in the development of money or currency around 3,000 years ago (33), which then opened the door for individuals to amass currency.

If you thumb backwards a few pages, you will see the discussion in the previous chapter about the bioevolutionary origins of fear and how we manage our fear behaviorally. At this point I hope it has become obvious that the necessity for engaging in survival-oriented activities to ward off fear is relatively common.

Regarding our discussion of social symptoms of fear gone awry, one of the most common manifestations behaviorally is what I've labeled "proactive-aggressive" fear, which is akin to the "fight" response of the fight-flight-freeze process biologists and psychologists use to conceptualize animal fear resolution strategies. I propose that our proactive-aggressive fear resolution strategy underlies greed. I guess the next question would be why do we need to engage in this strategy nowadays?

I think the common belief in most cultures goes something like this: if I have more money my life will generally be better. Well, let's take a step back and survey the global landscape and see why that belief might get hijacked by fear.

We now have rapid development of social communication and other technology, which is speeding up how quickly we conduct business (i.e., economic growth) as well as social expectations about how quickly we amass wealth (i.e., keeping up with the Joneses phenomenon). Moreover, there have been dramatic increases in intercultural contact, which can reasonably be a cause for socially-induced fear—see the religion argument above.

With the world population growth rate increasing (34), it simply means more people need to consume more resources more quickly, which requires more money, which in turn fuels the supply and demand dynamic discussed by economists. If you combine these factors, it would make sense that more people wish to accumulate more wealth at every level of socioeconomic strata (SES).

More money typically equates to more agency and freedom to enjoy life. I imagine lower SES individuals would like more financial security as well as a better standard of living, whereas moderate to high SES individuals wish to have an even nicer standard of living and increase their social capital. Still, how does this turn into what is being described here as greed?

When we think about greed, typically, we associate such conniving and selfish behavior with large corporations, especially those focused on selling us goods and services. But is it fair to pin the greed phenomenon on big business? I dare say no, and the rationale is simple.

If we consider greed, and not wealth accumulation, as a kind of hedonistically fear-driven phenomenon with the goal of thriving at the *expense* of others' welfare, then it stands to reason that anyone who selfishly hoards money or usurps money is contributing to the greed problem.

Now, economics is a tricky science. To give a theoretical example and adequately describe all the social and economic forces would not be pragmatic for the purposes of this work. The idea of hoarding money implies that said money is not being spent on necessary or important goods, services, or people.

So, a billion-dollar corporation would be considered greedy if a reasonable percent of the profit was not spent on necessities like employees' salaries, insurance, product improvement, infrastructure investment, employee wellness needs, or maintaining a *fair and healthy relationship with their customers* (i.e., providing reasonable services that customers need and not conning customers). The perfect example of this big business greed process is the housing bubble bursting in the U.S. in 2008 due to the subprime mortgage catastrophe (35).

The short-term gains (i.e., greed) desired by bankers at major companies, investment firms, and real-estate developers nicely commingled and resulted in mortgage offerings to individuals who wanted to capitalize on their fear-driven desire to "have a better life" (i.e., greedily trying to live beyond one's means with a bigger or nicer house). This resulted in thousands defaulting on their mortgages due to questionably-structured mortgage/payment plans as well as insufficient funds on the part of the banks and buyers. Both parties were guilty of greed in that example.

In the same way, it would be fair to consider an individual of lower socioeconomic status greedy if said individual were to avoid spending their money on necessities for themselves or their children, and instead selfishly engaged in hedonistic behaviors (e.g., drinking, smoking, gambling, or buying nice clothing) or simply just tucked the money away without a plan for saving.

This can all be considered greedy behavior. Greed is the outgrowth of fear gone awry. We spend too much time keeping up with the Joneses and too little time meditating and budgeting out our financial needs. As the Oxford Dictionary definition states, greed is not only about wealth, but also commonly revolves around issues of power or accumulation of goods.

If any of us were to begin amassing goods, such as food, at the expense of the people in a given area, then we might consider that greed as well. For decades now researchers have been following the behavior of survivors of the Holocaust during World War II and what they have found is fascinating. A significant percentage of Holocaust survivors, as well as those from other traumatic enslavement and prejudicial social thinning, have been found to hoard food (36, 37), though there is some controversy about how often this happens (38).

Why? Well, because the traumatic nature of starvation and having one's life threatened altered these individual's stress responses (i.e., fear response) (39). Now, when you think of a stereotypical picture of a Holocaust survivor, I'm sure you aren't imagining someone greedily keeping food at the expense of their family or community's welfare, right?

Food hoarding is, after all, a relatively common phenomenon in the animal kingdom and it tends to be adaptive because it helps us develop specialized survival memory faculties (40). The truth is, however, this desire to amass food is driven by an irreparably altered fear system in Holocaust survivors.

It makes sense that if the object of your fear for years on end was whether you would be fed by your captors or not, eventually your natural fear response related to hunger pains would get hijacked and overwhelmed by the circumstances. It's akin to your car being stuck in high gear going 80 miles per hour, even though you are stepping on the breaks in a 20 mile-per-hour zone because the accelerator software in your car's computer is broken.

Do we consider Holocaust survivors "greedy?" Absolutely not. The hoarding of food has negligible consequences for the individual and their family compared to the massive personal and societal consequences seen in the 2008 subprime mortgage crisis. Technically, both are greed behaviors, and both are driven by fear.

The general point is that our fear-driven need to keep money at the expense of our own or another's wellbeing is a problem. When we observe others being greedy, we in turn then become hijacked by fear and engage in quasi-greed driven behavior or hoarding behavior to counter greed, which in turn creates societal conflict and perpetuates fear.

Summary

A lot of ground has been covered in this chapter. I have made the argument thus far that we have an evolutionarily adaptive fear response, a normal biological reaction to perceived or actual threats. While this natural biological reaction is mostly adaptive, we have changed so much as a species that our circumstances have afforded us a more complex and quicker way of living.

I propose that when humans functioned in more primal and tribal ways, which still exist as social or cultural norms in some parts of the world, having a more fear-driven way of being helped us evolve and survive successfully. The premise here is that, although we were designed and have been socialized to function in more primal ways, our current global climate combined with the advances in technology, education, human rights, and morality require a more sophisticated approach to our fear response. Specifically, I propose that our fear response has been hijacked or co-opted by four phenomena: technology, politics, religion, and greed.

Technology, politics, religion, and greed all serve, or have served, a very adaptive purpose in our world. Technology and greed have afforded such intense connection and rapid sociocultural and economic development that society is advancing at a pace like we have never seen before in recorded history. The problem, however, is that such intense connection and such rapid change means we are exposed to each other more often and learn more quickly, which relates to the next two problems.

Regarding religion and politics, the basic problem is the same—that these two methods of social-relating and negotiating are based upon more tribalistic (i.e., us versus them) ways of relating, which will always cause fear-based divisiveness and result in ostracism or aggression. The inherent problem with tribalism in most parts of the world is that we simply do not culturally or socially function that way anymore.

Although we are biologically programmed to live in a quasi-tribalistic manner because it helped us survive, it seems as if global society—not to be confused with globalism—is moving away from our evolutionary urge for tribalism. As we learn more, relate more quickly, and advance in more sophisticated ways thanks to technology, our more primitive brain is left in the dust.

This means we are at a crucial point in our evolutionary and cultural development. We need to learn how to adapt to our changing circumstances. I am not advocating, however, that we simply give up on religion, politics, making money, or creating new and exciting technology.

I'm not saying we should all hold hands and sing "Kumbaya." I'm simply hoping we can begin to have an intellectually honest discussion about how much our fear response has been both hijacked by, and left in the dust by, these four phenomena.

At the end of this book I will propose some concrete and simple methods for either de-escalating the fear hijacking or helping our evolutionary instinct "catch up" to our current rate of development. In the meantime, I would like to take the opportunity to outline the consequences of our unchecked fear for us all, starting with the consequences to ourselves as individuals.

REFERENCES

1. Patchin, J.W. (2013). Cyberbullying research: 2013 update. Retrieved on September 27th, 2016 from: http://cyberbullying.org/cyberbullying-research-2013-update

2. Siegel, D.J. (2011). *Mindsight: The New Science of Personal Transformation*. New York, NY: Bantam Books.

3. Marie Claire. (2016). This is the Most Liked Instagram Photo. Retrieved on September 27th, 2016 from: http://www.marieclaire.co.uk/news/celebrity-news/most-liked-instagram-photo-29093

4. Lang, C. (2016). This is the New Most-Liked Instagram Photo. Retrieved on September 27th, 2016 from: http://time.com/4320988/most-liked-instagram-selena-bomez-justin-bieber/

5. American Psychiatric Association (2014). *The Diagnostic and Statistical Manual of Mental Disorders*. (5th, Ed.).

6. Chang, L. (2015). Americans spend an alarming amount of time checking social media on their phones. Retrieved on September 27th, 2016 from: http://www.digitaltrends.com/mobile/informate-report-social-media-smartphone-use/

7. Panksepp, J. (1998). *Affective Neuroscience: The Foundations of Human and Animal Emotions*. New York: Oxford University Press.

8. STATISTA. (2017). Percentage of the us population with a social network profile. Retrieved on September 27th, 2016 from: https://www.statista.com/statistics/273476/percentage-of-us-population-with-a-social-networkprofile/

9. Lane, M. (2016). *The Birth of Politics: Eight Greek and Roman Political Ideas and Why They Matter*. Princeton, NJ: Princeton University Press

10. Kaplan, J.T., Gambel, S.I., & Harris, S. (2016). Neural correlates of one's political beliefs in the face of counterevidence. *Scientific Reports (6)*. doi:10.1038/srep39589

11. Gerher, G. (2016). Black-and-White Thinking In Our Social Worlds: The Evolutionary Basis of Simple Thinking. Retrieved on September 27th, 2016 from: https://www.psychologytoday.com/blog/darwins-subterranean-world/201601/black-and-white-thinking-in-our-social-worlds

12. The Social Progress Imperative (2016). Data definitions. Retrieved on September 27th, 2016 from: http://www.socialprogressimperative.org/global-index/data-definitions/

13. National Coalition for the Homelessness. (2014). LGBT homelessness. Retrieved on September 27th, 2016 from: http://nationalhomeless.org/issues/lgbt/

14. Encyclopedia Britannica. (2016). Don't Ask, Don't Tell. Retrieved on September 27th, 2016 from: https://www.britannica.com/event/Dont-Ask-Dont-Tell

15. United States Supreme Court. (2014). OBERGEFELL ET AL. v. HODGES, DIRECTOR,

OHIO DEPARTMENT OF HEALTH, ET AL: CERTIORARI TO THE UNITED STATES COURT OF APPEALS FOR THE SIXTH CIRCUIT Retrieved on September 27th, 2016 from: https://www.supremecourt.gov/opinions/14pdf/14-556_3204.pdf

16.   United States Equal Employment Opportunity Commission. (2016). What you should know about EEOC and the enforcement protections for LGBT workers. Retrieved on September 27th, 2016 from: https://www.eeoc.gov/eeoc/newsroom/wysk/enforcement_protections_lgbt_workers.cfm

17.   Bailey, J., Wallace, M., & Wright, B. (2013). Are gay men and lesbians discriminated against when applying for jobs? A four-city, internet-based field experiment. *Journal of Homosexuality, 60*(6), 873-894.

18.   Bauermeister, J. A., Meanley, S., Hickok, A., Pingel, E., VanHemert, W., & Loveluck, J. (2014). Sexuality-related work discrimination and its association with the health of sexual minority emerging and young adult men in the Detroit metro area. *Sexuality Research & Social Policy: A Journal of the NSRC, 11*(1), 1-10.

19.   Rios, D., & Eaton, A. (2016). Perceived Social Support in the Lives of Gay, Bisexual and Queer Hispanic College Men. *Culture, Health & Sexuality, 18*(10), 1093-1106.

20.   Van Sluytman, L., Spikes, P., Nandi, V., Van Tieu, H., Frye, V., Patterson, J., & Koblin, B. (2015). Ties that bind: Community attachment and the experience of discrimination among black men who have sex with men. *Culture, Health & Sexuality, 17*(7), 859-872.

21.   Johns, M. M., Pingel, E. S., Youatt, E. J., Soler, J. H., Mcclelland, S. I., & Bauermeister, J. A. (2013). LGBT community, social network characteristics, and smoking behaviors in young sexual minority women. *American Journal of Community Psychology, 52*(1-2), 141-54.

22.   Human Rights Campaign. (2016). Growing up LGBT in America. Retrieved on September 27th, 2016 from: http://www.hrc.org/youth-report/view-and-share-statistics

23.   Shapiro, L. (2015). Record number of reported LGBT homicides in 2015 so far. *Huffington Post.* Retrieved on September 27th, 2016 from: http://www.huffingtonpost.com/2015/04/02/lgbt-homicides_n_6993484.html

24.   Unknown (2014). Scientists claim that Quantum Theory proves consciousness moves to another universe at death. *Signs of The Times.* Retrieved on September 27th, 2016 from: https://www.sott.net/article/271933-Scientists-claim-that-Quantum-Theory-proves-consciousness-moves-to-another-universe-at-death

25.   Carroll, S.M. (2011). Physics and the immortality of the soul. *Scientific American.* Retrieved on September 27th, 2016 from: https://blogs.scientificamerican.com/guest-blog/physics-and-the-immortality-of-the-soul/

26.   Nauert, R. (2016). "Herd" Mentality Explained. *Psych Central.* Retrieved on September 27th, 2016 from: http://psychcentral.com/news/2008/02/15/herd-mentality-explained/1922.html

27.   Russell, B., 1912, "The Philosophy of Bergson," *The Monist,* 22: 321–347.

28.   Thapa, S.J. & Freedberg, J. (2015). Equality rising: Global equality report. (Cobb, T., Fowler, A., Hughes, J., & Wood, M. Eds). Retrieved on September 27th, 2016 from: http://hrc-assets.s3-website-us-east-1.amazonaws.com//files/assets/resources/EqualityRising-2015-052016.pdf

29.   American Psychological Association. (2017). Lesbian, gay, bisexual and transgender persons &

socioeconomic status. Retrieved on September 27th, 2016 from: http://www.apa.org/pi/ses/resources/publications/lgbt.aspx

30. Zhong, W., Cristofori, I., Bulbulia, J., Krueger, F., & Grafman, J. (2017). Biological and cognitive underpinnings of religious fundamentalism. *Neuropsychologia, 100*, 18-25.

31. Collier, P. & Hoeffler, A. (2004). Greed and grievance in civil war. *Oxford Economic Papers*, 56(4), 563-595.

32. Oxford University Press (2017). Greed: definition. Retrieved on January 1st, 2017 from: https://en.oxforddictionaries.com/definition/greed

33. Beattie, A. (2015). The history of money: From barter to banknotes. Retrieved on January 8th, 2017 from: http://www.investopedia.com/articles/07/roots_of_money.asp

34. Garfield, L. (2016). The world's population is growing faster than we thought. Retrieved on February 2nd, 2017 from: http://www.sciencealert.com/the-world-s-population-is-growing-faster-than-we-thought-new-report-finds

35. Denning, S. (2011). Lest we forget: Why we had a financial crisis. Retrieved on February 4th from: http://www.forbes.com/sites/stevedenning/2011/11/22/5086/#3ea8e3de5b56

36. Tress, L. (2016). For many holocaust survivors, effects of wartime starvation still a plague. *The Times of Israel.* Retrieved on April 6th, 2016 from: https://www.statista.com/statistics/273476/percentage-of-us-population-with-a-social-networkprofile/

37. Brown, K.D. (2012). Recognizing delayed pstd in holocaust survivors: Decades after wwii, many show signs of delayed post-traumatic stress disorder. Retrieved on April 6th, 2016 from: https://www.bostonglobe.com/lifestyle/health-wellness/2012/06/10/recognizing-delayedptsd-holocaust-survivors/NmVaT4wUO3GZj0czLYab0L/story.html

38. Bachar, E., Canetti, L., & Berry, E.M. (2005). Lack of Long-Lasting Consequences of Starvation on Eating Pathology in Jewish Holocaust Survivors of Nazi Concentration Camps. *Journal of Abnormal Psychology*, *114*(1). 165-169.

39. Rodriguez, T. (2015). Descendants of holocaust survivors have altered stress hormones: Parents' traumatic experience may hamper their offspring's ability to bounce back from trauma. Retrieved on April 6th, 2016 from: https://www.scientificamerican.com/article/descendants-of-holocaust-survivors-have-alteredstress-hormones/

40. Pravosudov, V.V. & Roth II, T.C. (2013). Cognitive ecology of food hoarding: The evolution of spatial memory and the hippocampus. Annual Review of Ecology, Evolution, and Systematics, 44(1). https://DOI:10.1146/annurev-ecolsys-110512135904m

"Unexpressed emotions will never die. They are buried alive and will come forth later in uglier ways."

SIGMUND FREUD

CHAPTER 4:
CONSEQUENCES TO THE INDIVIDUAL

F reud's quote seems to be right on for our discussion about fear. The foundation has been laid for understanding how fear works in a very basic manner. It's time to make that case that unchecked fear, the process of allowing our socially-learned fears to remain, has consequences for us all on every level of interpersonal and intrapersonal functioning. The simplest place to start on our journey of exploring how unchecked fear affects us all is to discuss the implications of not dealing with personal fear daily.

Thus far, I've discussed some examples of personal experiences of fear gone awry. However, I think it would be wise to highlight the most likely common categories/situations wherein we all struggle with unchecked fear individually. I propose that there are three common consequences to individuals as result of our unchecked fear problem: increased interpersonal conflict leading to decreased social connection, loss of intellectual honesty, and maladaptive coping patterns as a result.

Increased Interpersonal Conflict

The first and most compelling problem that our unchecked fear poses to all of us as individuals is a direct increase in interpersonal conflict. My reasoning for saying excess fear leads to conflict is simple; it just makes sense. Because we experience more fear more intensely more often, we are less likely to have appropriate coping skills and be utilizing them because we have more fear.

It's not as if the world is suddenly much scarier than it used to be 50 or even 100 years ago. There are still the same out-groups and disparate ideologies that threaten your way of life. We simply have more awareness of and less interest in dealing with the root of the problem, as discussed in the social phenomenon chapter.

If you thumb back a few pages to the previous chapter, I outlined how the four major drivers of our unchecked fear (i.e., politics, greed, religion, and speedy technological advancement) promote interpersonal conflict using specific examples. I propose that there is an increase in interpersonal conflict because of our increased rate of interpersonal connection.

Why? Well, because a significant portion of our modern interpersonal connection comes through technology, we naturally have so many more opportunities to relate to each other much more quickly and frequently and discuss so many more "hot button" topics. This is the perfect formula for increased interpersonal conflict.

A + B = C.

A= Increased **A**ccess to new people/cultures/ideas/technology that cause us to...

B= **B**elieve we aren't safe (i.e., legitimately feeling threatened by actual threats we learn of) OR that challenges our ideals/way of life (e.g., recalcitrance of beliefs, tribalism, identity politics, movement formation/ development of social justice groups), which represents our *illegitimate* fear of safety and leads to...

C= More **C**onflict with friends, coworkers, family members, and people we don't even know.

For instance, think about your personal life for the last year. Think about your relationships. If you've lived in the United States, Europe, or Asia there have been so many political, religious, economic, and social conflicts that have arisen—many of them due to conflicting views about world leaders like President Donald Trump.

Think about the number of discussions or arguments you have had in the past year about politics, social justice issues, or economics. I bet, if you tallied up all the arguments about just those four topics—not including more personal arguments—it would total upwards of two hundred, if not more. If you scroll back to pre-social media times, heck pre-internet times, I would be willing to bet there were fewer arguments about these issues—or at least less intense arguments because life was (seemingly) simpler and more predictable because we simply did not know about the various conflicts.

Essentially, the more we are in contact and the more we learn about things that cause conflict, or legitimate fear, the more we engage in emotionally intense and biased discussions (i.e., arguments). Now, I cannot prove that we argue more now compared to 10 years ago or 100 years ago, frankly because I have not been able to find valid polls or research studies conducted on this topic. I will, however, assert that we likely argue more frequently nowadays because of the reasons described above.

Our desire to argue serves two purposes: tension relief and hope for change. Every time we argue, we are likely feeling a sense of anxiety or anger. One of the most normal ways of getting relief from feelings is by talking about them with other people because this engenders a sense of feeling heard by the other—a normal conflict resolution need (1) which typically promotes a sense of agency (2).

Our sense of agency is driven by our belief that our actions will reliably provide relief or produce a useful change, although it's not necessarily true that we can meaningfully affect our environment to the degree that one would prefer (3). Although arguing might provide temporary relief because you believe that you have impacted the other person's opinion or behavior, it does not fully relieve your fear.

For example, arguing with a friend about their political opinion does not change the overall political problem the two of you are engaged in an argument about. The problem is our sense of agency showcased in arguing is really a hedonistic exercise (i.e., emotional vomiting), and not really showcasing morality and coherence (4) because it shows a lack of respect for both yourself and the person on whom you are vomiting your fear.

If we engage in arguing, it automatically puts the other person on the defensive, which will not likely help the cause and will cyclically reinforce fear. I think this arguing phenomenon results in a cyclical process of verbal fear vomiting, conflict, and disconnection, and disconnection is the enemy. Arguing about ideas or circumstances is different than a healthy discourse, which I will discuss in the solutions chapter.

Loss of Intellectual Honesty

Due to living in a fear-based mindset, it seems as if all people, regardless of critical thinking capacity or IQ, are reasoning less honestly than in prior generations or in simpler times. I have heard authors like Sam Harris (5) and others mention in their articles and podcasts a similar belief in this current problem.

Given all that is happening in the political scene, it seems like we have more and more examples of bad models for intellectual honesty, and the more we have seemingly dishonest leaders, the more a culture tends to engage in intellectual dishonesty (6). Unfortunately, I cannot support my rationale for this fear consequence with any fact-based claims or statistics on the increase of intellectually dishonest discourse in the U.S. or in other cultures. This is simply both my experience as well as the reported experience of many of my colleagues and acquaintances.

The one tangible fact that somewhat supports my belief that we have lost more of our ability to be intellectually honest is the recent development of "fake news" scandals and stories. If the entire gambit of journalists, from major news organizations to lesser known opinion writers, have been disseminating "fake news," or unnecessarily biased stories that mislead people with unsubstantiated ideas, it stands to reason that our fear has driven us to a place of desperation to prove our point and ignore other facts that contradict our point of view.

What exactly do I mean by intellectual honesty? When using this phrase, I am describing a way of reasoning that goes beyond simple logic or simple skepticism—though skepticism would go a long way in righting the problems we face. I'm proposing that we need to reason in a more honest manner.

Simple logic goes like this: Because "A" happened, then "B" must be true. However, dozens of factors can account for what happened in "A" or caused result "B." This can be exemplified in any overly simplistic thought. For example, there is a stereotype that African Americans in the U.S. are more often violent, with some research showing that African American youth are more often violent (7).

So, a simple fact-based seemingly logical expression that might show up in conversation goes like this. If African Americans are more violent, then it's likely that they're more responsible for, or more often involved in, violent crime. Looking at other statistics might also confirm this at first glance because, for instance, African Americans in the U.S. were murdered more often by African Americans than any other racial group (8); therefore African Americans must be more violent as a race.

This conclusion is simply not true for so many reasons. If you look up the FBI report from 2013, which I cited in my theoretical race example, you will see first and foremost that there were more Caucasian murders, committed by predominantly Caucasians, than there were murders of African Americans.

We also do not know about the number of unreported assaults, bar fights, and other violent acts that are never handled by the police, never reported. It would also be good to know if this statistic was true in previous years, or more recently. Moreover, is this statistic just true here in the U.S. or is it true around the world?

There are so many facts that we simply do not know. A more intellectually honest argument would look at violent crime rates, murder rates, and assaults, among other things, over a long period of time all over the globe to see if violence is more common among one race or another—as opposed to focusing on just one type of statistic at one time. Then couple this research with an honest hedge about the sources of the facts and what is also not known at the conclusion. This is the kind of argument that is missing in modern discourse nowadays.

I believe that we are more interested in picking a side and not thoroughly evaluating that side's argument. We are especially disinterested in any kind of skepticism about our own beliefs because it causes cognitive dissonance and elicits fear, which is an assertion now being supported by research in the social sciences (9).

A desire to fit in and be a part of an ideology or social cause, which is not inherently bad, is nowadays more driven by bad logic and a desire to look good at the expense of being honest. I propose that the more fear we experience, and the less we deal with it, then the more we push to prove our point (or our group's point)—even when we have no substantive proof.

If you recall chapter 2's section on the brain and fear, the research shows that when we experience fear our frontal cortices (i.e., thinking, reasoning, and planning areas of the brain) are more "off-line," and, ironically, when we are stressed or experiencing fear we automatically access parts of the brain responsible for automatic responding and reflexive (not detailed) memories like what is seen in flashbacks and PTSD (10, 11).

Excessive fear limits our ability to reason honestly and makes us respond in a more reactionary—non-mindful or thoughtful—manner; therefore, when we're afraid and trying to prove a point, we're not as able to be intellectually honest. This is a cyclical process of feeling fear, which promotes intellectual dishonesty, which promotes arguments that aren't sound, which draws criticism from others, which makes us feel excluded, which makes us feel afraid because people poke holes in our arguments, which keeps us on the defensive, which keeps us from thinking clearly. We need to break the cycle, which I will discuss in the solutions chapter.

Maladaptive Coping

Born out of fear, with all of this arguing and not thinking clearly, we are eventually going to do something to alleviate our fear. Given the lack of intellectual honesty and increase in interpersonal conflict, our typical circumstances for finding relief (i.e., in healthy discussion in relationships) are not at our disposal as reliably as we need them to be.

With this in mind, I'd say it makes sense that we have seen an upswing in maladaptive methods of coping with our fear all over the world.

Generally, the most normal response to feeling overwhelmed is a sort of checking out from reality, which is what my colleagues might call dissociation, denial, or avoidance. Each of these labels implies a degree of pathology and a maladaptive process.

For the purposes of our discussion, let's just call it "checking out" so that the entire spectrum of more adaptive to less adaptive, more pathological to less pathological, can be covered. We all check out in various ways at various times for both good reasons and bad reasons. I believe that we have taken to checking out more often, in Western cultures in particular, due to our widespread fear problem.

I'm equating checking out with maladaptive coping here because, as I hope to prove, we're checking out more often and in more problematic ways. Regarding our maladaptive coping problem, it seems like there are two predominant methods that modern man has begun relying on to check out: drug/alcohol use and excessive consumption of television, media, social media.

Addictions

If you scroll through news articles, Facebook posts, and blog posts over the past 10 years, you would see a dramatic increase in the number of stories describing some new thing as addictive or a resurgence in worry about how addictive foods and other substances are. It's not an incredulous leap in logic to discuss the drug epidemic and obesity epidemics as related to our increased experiences of fear.

For example, according to the National Institute of Drug Abuse, the overall national trends indicate increased drug and alcohol use, with large jumps in drug use rates by individuals aged 50-60 (12). Addiction is a huge issue in the United States, costing us over $700 billion each year (13). Moreover, a recent article showed that the rate of heroin overdose quadrupled in the last five years (14).

In the past 20 years, we've also developed many new kinds of addictions like compulsive shopping, exercising, technology, and sex. Some of these wouldn't have existed without technology, and others have been readily available (i.e., sex addiction and exercise addiction). We can quibble over whether these addictions represent the same kind of national health crisis as heroin or alcohol; however, the general principle is that we've developed all sorts of compulsive habits that keep us disengaged from healthy relationships and subsequently emotionally checked out. Interesting side note: a man in Japan died from his sex addiction because his outrageously large collection of pornographic magazines fell and crushed him to death (15).

To be clear, I am not proposing that addiction is caused by fear. Addiction is defined as a maladaptive and compulsive use of drugs, alcohol, and other substances, and its behaviors are complex. To fully understand the development of addiction, we would need to discuss genetics, brain development, attachment, affect regulation issues, and cultural issues, which is outside the scope of this work. I do propose, however, that addiction is a means of checking out (i.e., of regulating our emotional states).

It makes sense, therefore, that because we are so much more engaged in fear nowadays, so much more often hijacked by our unreasonable social pressures and intellectually dishonest beliefs, we have a more intense and more consistent desire to check out or dissociate.

It's also reasonable to believe that because we are working so hard to keep up with today's fast-paced society, we might use drugs or alcohol to "enhance" productivity (16), but the fact that it's only enhancing and serves in no way to help de-escalate stress/fear is debatable. The general point is that we're checking out more now than in the past by compulsively using substances and maladaptive behaviors.

Excessive Consumption of Media

Generally, since the birth of television and movies, we have had a delightful way of entertaining ourselves and a healthy distraction (17). I would wager, however, that our delightful distraction has become a bigger part of our lives than we are aware. For instance, the average person will spend about four hours per day watching television, which totals out to nine years over the course of their life (18, 19). Moreover, 49 percent of people surveyed in those studies said they watched too much television.

So what do these numbers mean? To be intellectually honest, one study showed that people between the ages of 18-24 are watching less TV nowadays compared to a few years ago (20). However, though teens are watching less TV, it's fair to assume that time has been devoted to other outlets...like social media.

The most recent academic or research-informed opinion on teenagers and social media is saddening. It seems as if teens are literally co-creating an engulfing and damaging environment of electronic connection because it's immediately rewarding, which has grown to the point where teens are now using texting and other social media/electronic media methods and prefer it more than any other kind of communication (21).

Although we're attempting to connect more by constantly updating our Facebook, Twitter, Instagram, or Snapchat, I also believe that we're really attempting to "check out" from ourselves and our own problems. For instance, the average internet user around the world spends about 118 minutes engaged in social media per day (22), which is likely higher in industrialized countries. That's almost two hours on average.

Moreover, people are watching seven million videos per minute on Snapchat and sending about 3.5 million texts per minute (23). Our social media consumption is clearly spinning out of control because in 2005 only 5 percent of the population used social media, which grew to 50 percent in 2011. As of January 2017 between 70-80 percent of people in the U.S. actively use a social media profile (24, 25). Most people in the U.S. are literally spending two hours of the day on social media, which could instead be spent connecting with loved ones, working out, or meditating.

I propose that all this time online results in one specific negative consequence: more pain. More time spent on social networking sites and apps means less face time with people. This is particularly problematic in my opinion because, again, we're biologically programmed to want to connect in a real and meaningful way with others. Although there is an aspect of meaningfulness to spending time and sharing with each other on social media, it is not nearly as "real" or as intensely meaningful due to the virtual nature of the connection (26)–though some might wish to philosophically debate this point, which I welcome!

Given that we're connecting less often in "real" ways, we're likely feeling lonelier as individuals, which would reasonably cause us to cope in a maladaptive manner to deal with the psychological pain of disconnection (27). That may sound somewhat dramatized, but think about it: If the rate of opioid (i.e., a pain medication) abuse has steadily gone up in this country, is it really that unreasonable to believe that our more technologically-induced isolationist lifestyle plays no part in it?

For decades now, we've been experiencing greater and more consistent disconnection, which means we likely are feeling more pain due to said disconnection. This is a topic I would greatly appreciate the chance to discuss with anyone. Given the understanding of our social connection/pain system as of the point in 2017 when I was writing this, I propose that our drug, alcohol, and other maladaptive coping behaviors through sex, technology, and obsessing over social media will continue to be on the rise because of our increased disconnection from each other, whether it be because we're simply looking at screens too often while in the company of others, or, whether our technology use is simply keeping us isolated and less reliant on in-person or face-to-face connection.

Summary

The long and the short of my argument here is simple: our hijacked (i.e., over-sensitive and overactive) fear response has led us to disconnect more, reason less honestly, and cope more compulsively. The sad thing is that these three adaptations to our hijacked fear response do not solve the problem.

It stands to reason that social disconnection, poor reasoning, and compulsive behavior only make us feel worse, which then cyclically reinforces our hijacked fear response. Due to the fact that the biggest consequence to us as individuals from our hijacked fear response is a feeling of making things worse, there is a negative view in our cultures and the countries in which we live of said feeling (i.e., psychological pain), which will be discussed in the next chapter.

REFERENCES

1.   Bruneu, E.G. & Saxe, R. (2012). The power of being heard: The benefits of 'perspective-giving' in the context of intergroup conflict. *The Journal of Experimental Social Psychology, 48*(4), 855-866.

2.   Stanford Encyclopedia of Philosophy. (2015). Agency. (Schlosser, M., Ed.). Retrieved on February 2nd, 2017 from: https://plato.stanford.edu/entries/agency/

3.   Haggard, P. & Tsakiris, M. (2009). The experience of agency: Feelings, judgments, and responsibility. *Current Directions in Psychological Science, 18*(4), 242-246.

4.   Geiger, I. (2011) "Rational Feelings and Moral Agency", *Kantian Review, 16*(2), pp. 283–308. doi: 10.1017/S1369415410000038.

5.   Harris, S. (2016). What Scientific Term or Concept Ought to be More Widely Known? Edge.org. Retrieved on March 4th, 20017 from: https://www.edge.org/response-detail/27227

6.   Makin, S. (2017). National corruption breeds personal dishonesty. *Scientific American.* Retrieved on March 22nd, 2017 from: https://www.scientificamerican.com/article/national-corruption-breeds-personal-dishonesty/?WT.mc_id=SA_FB_MB_FEAT

7.   Bushman, B.J., et al. (2015). Youth violence: What we know and what we need to know. *American Psychologist, 71*, 17-39.

8.   U.S. Department of Justice. (2014). Crime in the United States: Expanded homicide data table 6. Retrieved on March 3rd, 207 from: https://ucr.fbi.gov/crime-in-the-u.s/2013/crime-in-the-u.s.-2013/offenses-known-to-law-enforcement/expanded-homicide/expanded_homicide_data_table_6_murder_race_and_sex_of_vicitm_by_race_and_sex_of_offender_2013.xls

9.   Frimer, J.A., Skitka, L.J., & Motyl, M. (2017). Liberals and Conservatives are Similarly Motivated to Avoid Exposure to One Another's Opinions. *Journal of Experimental Social Psychology, 72*, 1-12.

10. Arnsten, A.F.T., Rasking, M.A., Taylor, F.B., & Connor, D.F. (2015). The Effects of Stress Exposure on Prefrontal Cortex: Translating Basic Research into Successful Treatments for Post-Traumatic Stress Disorder. *Neurobiology of Stress, 1*, 89-99.

11. Schwabe, L. (2017). Memory under stress: From single system to network changes. *European Journal of Neuroscience, 45*(4), 478-489.

12. NIDA (2015). Drugfacts: Nationwide trends. Retrieved on March 11th, 2017 from: https://www.drugabuse.gov/publications/drugfacts/nationwide-trends

13. NIDA (2015). Trends & statistics. Retrieved on March 1st, 2017 from: https://www.drugabuse.gov/related-topics/trends-statistics

14. Beasly, D. (2017). Deadly U.S. Heroin overdoses quadrupled in 5 years. *Scientific American.* Retrieved on March 2nd, 2017 from: https://www.scientificamerican.com/article/deadly-u-s-heroin-overdoses-quadrupled-in-5-years/

15.   Nsubuga, J. (2017). Man in Japan dies after his massive porn collection falls on him. Retrieved on March 10th, 2017 from: http://metro.co.uk/2017/03/03/man-dies-after-his-massive-porn-magazine-collection-falls-on-him-6486367/?ito=facebook

16.   Friedman, N., Orwig, J., & Kakoyiannis, A. (2017). People in California are microdosing on LSD—and they say it's making them more productive. Business Insider. Retrieved on March 10th, 2017 from: http://www.businessinsider.com/silicon-valley-chris-kilham-medicine-hunter-microdosing-lsd-acid-microdose-productive-2017-1?utm_content=buffere9e5c&utm_medium=social&utm_source=facebook.com&utm_campaign=buffer-bi

17.   Rubin, A. (2002). The uses-and-gratifications perspective of media effects. In J. Bryand & D. Zillman (Eds.). *Media effects: Advances in theory and research*. (2nd ed., pp .525-548). Mahwah, NJ: Earlbaum.

18.   California State University Northridge (2007). Television & health. (Herr, N., Ed.). Retrieved on March 2nd, 2017 from: https://www.csun.edu/science/health/docs/tv&health.html

19.   Statistics Brain (2016). Television watching statistics. Retrieved on March 2nd, 2017 from: http://www.statisticbrain.com/television-watching-statistics/

20.   Marketing Charts (2017). The state of traditional TV: Updated with Q3 2016 data. (Lupis, J.C., Ed.). Retrieved on March 2nd, 2017 from: http://www.marketingcharts.com/television/are-young-people-watching-less-tv-24817/

21.   Underwood, M.K. & Ehrenreich, S.E. (2017). The power and the pain of adolescents' digital communication: Cyber victimization and the perils of lurking. *American Psychologist*, 72(2), 144-158.

22.   Statista (2017). Global time spent on social networking by internet users worldwide from 2012 to 2016 (in minutes). Retrieved on March 2nd, 2017 from: https://www.statista.com/statistics/433871/daily-social-media-usage-worldwide/

23.   Statista (2016). Media usage in an internet usage as of June 2016. Retrieved on March 2nd, 2017 from: https://www.statista.com/statistics/195140/new-user-generated-content-uploaded-by-users-per-minute/

24.   Pew Research Center (2017). Social media fact sheet. Retrieved on March 8th, 2017 from: http://www.pewinternet.org/fact-sheet/social-media/

25.   Statista (2017). Percentage of the U.S. population with a social media profile from 2008 to 2017. Retrieved on March 10th, 2017 from: https://www.statista.com/statistics/273476/percentage-of-us-population-with-a-social-network-profile/

26.   Margalit, L. (2014). The psychology behind social media interactions: Why is digital communication so often easier than face-to-face. *Psychology Today*. Retrieved on March 23rd, 2017 from: https://www.psychologytoday.com/blog/behind-online-behavior/201408/the-psychology-behind-social-media-interactions

27.   Eisenberger, N.I. (2012). The pain of social disconnection: Examining the shared neural underpinnings of physical and social pain. *Nature Reviews Neuroscience*, 13, 421-434.

"People who think with their epidermis or their genitalia or their clan are the problem to begin with. One does not banish this specter by invoking it. If I would not vote against someone on the grounds of 'race' or 'gender' alone, then by the exact same token I would not cast a vote in his or her favor for the identical reason. Yet see how this obvious question makes fairly intelligent people say the most alarmingly stupid things."

CHRISTOPHER HITCHENS

CHAPTER 5:
CONSEQUENCES TO CULTURE

Up to this point, we've been discussing the consequences of a hijacked fear system for all of us as individuals, across our day-to-day experiences and in our relationships. I hope it has become abundantly clear that our unchecked fear has consistently negative consequences that lie on a spectrum from mildly problematic to emotionally or relationally destructive. Now, I think it would be useful to expand our understanding of how our fear affects not just our individual lives and circumstances, but also how our hijacked fear permeates up throughout different levels of broader and broader social dynamics.

The next level up from individual/interpersonal relating is cultural/subcultural relating. I'm using the word culture to describe any grouping of individuals based upon shared beliefs or characteristics, and not necessarily the more anthropological or social psychological term discussing nationality or ethnicity. There are three main consequences to our cultural dynamics that result from unchecked fear on an individual level: rigid tribalism, increased group conflict, and violence.

Rigid Tribalism

W ithin the fields of evolutionary psychology, anthropology, biology, and others, there have been 100 years of discussions about the development, utility, and maintenance of a concept called tribalism among various species, especially mammals. Tribalism can be defined literally as "tribal consciousness and loyalty" (1) or "the state or fact of being organized in a tribe or tribes" (2). Tribalism can also be more broadly defined as a "strong in-group loyalty" (1).

Most animals, especially mammals, operate in a tribalistic manner. Tribalism generally serves the purpose of keeping us safe from "outsiders," developing a sense of interpersonal identity, and having a familiar group with which to not feel lonely—we're not biologically designed to function asocially.

The concept of tribalism is very important for our dissection of how fear affects cultural systems. If you were to take a step back from your everyday life, you would find that you are a member of several tribes based upon concepts like: biological/fictive family, race/ethnicity, region of origin (i.e., state or country), educational status, employment type, religious affiliation, gender identity, or sexual identity as just a few examples.

For the most part, we self-identify based upon these concepts, with some out of our control—like where we were born and skin pigmentation— and others more in our control. What's important to note here is that people choose to self-identify based upon these concepts. This process of self-identification underlies the first cultural consequence born out of our fear problem—rigid tribalism.

When it comes to this concept of rigid tribalism I think we need to have an intellectually honest discussion about the difference between typical— non-problematic—tribalism versus rigid tribalism, which is consistently problematic nowadays. It makes the most sense to take this concept of tribalism and place it on a theoretical spectrum, which could look something like this:

Asocial Individualism | | Adaptive Group Identification | | Rigid Tribalism

This spectrum is a simplified way of viewing how people tend to identify as group members. On one end of the spectrum (i.e., asocial individualism) is the idea that a person almost pathologically avoids identification with groups, tribes, cultures, and kin. We might think of someone on this end of the spectrum as a kind of nihilistic psychopath, only "looking out for #1" and not caring about a group identity. In social psychology, this would be an extreme version of individualism, whereas rigid tribalism would be an extreme version of collectivism.

On the other end of the spectrum is rigid tribalism, which, in my mind, indicates a maladaptive adherence to a tribal identity (or to multiple tribal identities) to the point of losing focus on individualistic needs and free thinking. Rigid tribalism typically results in strong negative consequences, especially because people are afraid of losing people from their tribe, so they engage in bullying or other coercive behaviors (3).

Think back to the chapter on the four drivers of hijacked fear, specifically when I discussed technology and bullying. Tribalism creates "out-groups." Whenever there is an out-group, we automatically associate anyone who identifies with the out-group as representative of all the negative stereotypes, behaviors, and attitudes associated with that group. This is likely due to phenomenon studied in social psychology like the availability heuristic, confirmation bias, distinction bias, and the framing effect. Therefore, it seems as if we need a middle ground of some sort, which I've labeled *adaptive group identification*.

This idea of adaptive group identification I will discuss more in the chapter on solutions, but for the time being I'd like to introduce my rationale. There needs to be some balance in identifying with a group in a meaningful way that helps us feel a sense of belonging and safety without losing our ability to think independently and develop a critical opinion about the groups with which we identify.

This middle ground perspective, focusing on adaptive group identification and selection, is a source of contention (4) in the field of biology and evolutionary science because there are contrasting views about the adaptive utility of self-selecting in groups. Innately, as individuals, we are selfish (in a non-narcissistic sense) so that we and our genes survive better (5), and we will identify with and participate in groups to serve our attachment and physical survival needs in a patterned way.

The problem, however, is that our group selection and participation also requires a somewhat consistent pattern of self-sacrifice to some degree. Because of other social and genetic differences, we all do not operate in the same manner within a group. It is questionable that, with our diversity—even within a group with which we identify—that we truly self-select in an adaptive manner because group participation often results in negative consequences as well.

So, where does rigid tribalism come from? It's an overreaction to conflict and fear. It's a fair statement to say that we all have been functioning in a tribal manner since the dawn of time. As we have made advances in economics, science, medicine, social politics, and various other categories of knowledge, our tribes have been presented with opportunities to challenge the basic framework and functioning of the tribe.

If a tribe (i.e., culture, ideological group, religion, race, etc.) is faced with consistent conflict or threats, the tribe has two choices: modify function/ structure to adapt to changes or remain rigid to promote a false sense of homeostasis. It's this idea of maintaining irrational homeostasis—to borrow a biology term—or, more simply, "status quo" that promotes rigid tribalism. Therefore, there is a driving force underneath this desire to maintain the status quo, but what?

I propose that fear compels us to become rigid when in groups, as with the social psychology principles of groupthink (6) and confirmation bias (7). These two biases, and many others, affect the way we perceive information from the world and make decisions about how it fits with what builds group cohesion or feels "safe" in our tribe.

When we identify with a group, whether it be race, religion, nation, employment type, educational background, or what have you, we begin to feel as if the group represents who we are; it becomes part of our identity. When people or incidents challenge a group with which we identify, our evolutionarily appropriate response is fear because the fear will push us to react in such a way that will help our group or tribe survive.

Because the world is changing much faster, advancing and producing new knowledge, connecting at such a rapid pace, we are more often faced with contradictory or challenging information about the tribes with which we identify. Therefore, we are choosing to become more rigid in our tribal identification to maintain a sense of certainty and validity.

It seems as if our ability to normally function in quasi-cohesive tribes for the adaptive purpose of survival and success has turned into, or is increasingly becoming, a rigid identity process among many cultures or tribes within the global population. It's palpable considering the amount of fear that seems to just seep out of topics discussed on the news, in online communities, or on social media sites—the Brexit, nationalism versus globalism, the Machiavellian nature of various political leaders all over the world, terrorist organizations like ISIS, debates about "just how bad" one religion is compared to another, and so on. It appears that normal, healthy competition between tribes that leads to expectable (i.e., manageable) conflict is growing ever more intense with ever more disconnection between disparate ideology holders (i.e., tribes) so that now we have more social group conflict.

Group Conflict

If we build upon the individual consequences discussed in the last chapter, it makes even more sense that we seem to be experiencing so much more conflict both between and within groups or cultures. The lack of intellectual honesty combined with increased interpersonal conflict will logically lead to increased social group/cultural conflict. If we take a step back and survey the last five years of events of a military, political, and social justice nature, it seems as if we are experiencing an upswing in a more conflict-driven discourse about intergroup problems.

This theory is somewhat supported by the idea that all but 10 nations in the world are entangled some sort of diplomatic or military conflict (8). According to one study of global conflicts since the Cold War, the general number of conflicts is steadily on the rise since 2010, though fewer people are dying than in conflicts pre-Cold War era (9). From a non-military perspective, according to a Pew poll, people in the U.S.

find that the greatest source of conflict is politics at this point (10), with other typical conflicts still viewed as a huge problem (i.e., racial, age, and economic).

To further prove that cultures are in conflict increasingly more often, let's look at how news media is documenting this phenomenon. Many articles in the last few years have headlines mentioning "culture wars" and similar titles about categories such as music, politics, art, religion, and war (11-16). These mostly focus on blame and name calling, and they subsequently offer few, if any, substantive solutions. "Culture War" is a nicely evocative title that simply fuels people's tribalistic fear, continuing to create out-groups and drive us apart.

This culture war ideology in the media has escalated to the point where "Culture War" is now a search category in major papers like the *Huffington Post* (17). One columnist even detailed the modern history of culture wars showcasing how we have been discussing cultural differences and fighting with each other since the 60s; however, while things have progressed in some ways, we are still fighting over the same basic cultural ideologies in an unending and self-defeating manner (18). But why is this going to be unending?

Because we're not attacking the root of the problem: unmanaged fear and lack of critical thinking. For the past 50 years, different cultural groups in society have been "fighting" for freedom, equal treatment, autonomy, and respect with some success. However, the wounds of the past and the psychological damage of tribalistic fear from the past are not gone, but rather, getting worse.

One group is reacting to past injustices and current injustices from another group, and on and on, to the point where everyone feels afraid that they will either continue to be a victim or become an oppressor. Taking this evidence into account, it seems like the next most logical consequence of rigid tribalism and an increase in conflict is an increase in the number of violent acts.

Violence

The first, most obvious, example of an increase in culturally-based violence is the increase in the number of "terror" attacks. Again, the premise in chapter 3 is that phenomenon like technology, greed, and religion push our fear process into overdrive and create easier opportunities for fear-driven consequences. Well, when we think of modern-day terrorism, we're typically discussing either politically-motivated aggression or religiously-motivated attacks by groups like ISIS.

Given that premise, I want to discuss the raw data about the prevalence of terrorist attacks pre-technology and post-technology. The number of terror attacks has rapidly increased since the advent of the internet and our huge advances in travel, commerce, and weapons development. Combine this with tribalism (i.e., the intense spreading of religious and political ideologies) via social media, and now we have a much larger number of terrorist attacks.

So, here's the data. There were 635 attacks in 1970, 460 attacks in 1971, and 486 attacks in 1972 (19), which represented a steady trend up through the 80s and 90s. Fast-forward to the era of 9/11, in which we were just developing and refining our abilities to utilize technology like the Internet, and there were 1883 terrorist attacks.

In the last few years, since the advent of the biggest social media platforms, advances in online banking, and weapons development, the numbers have increased dramatically to where there were 4,784 attacks in 2010, 5,009 attacks in 2011, 8,498 attacks in 2012, 11,990 attacks in 2013, 16,840 attacks in 2014, and 14,806 attacks in 2015 (19). Take a step back and think about the dramatic difference from 1970 to 2014. The number of attacks increased from a few hundred to over 10,000 consistently. Hopefully this trend decreases.

A second way in which this fear hijacking process is affecting cultures and promoting violence involves the topic of culturally-motivated violence like racially-focused violence or other "hate" crimes. While the trends across various groups are inconsistent in their changes, the general rule of thumb for these various hate crimes is that more people are expressing their fear through violence as compared to the pre-internet era.

For instance, in England there were close to 45,000 hate crimes on record from 2013-2014, with the majority focused on race (20). Moreover, the number of hate groups is around 800; however, it hit its peak in 2011 at around 1,100, so the number is falling, but the number of hate groups is generally and steadily climbing up compared to the pre-internet era (21). This last source showed an interesting trend where here in the U.S. we have seen an increase in the number of religious hate crimes and a decrease in racial hate crime.

According to the FBI's statistics, most hate crimes by percentage are of a racial/ethnic nature (22), with around 6,000 incidents per year. In the U.S., the statistics indicate that approximately 7,000 people plus per year are killed or injured because of "hate," which I would argue is simply tribalism leading to violence.

One important caveat is that we have not been tracking hate crimes for very long in Western cultures. Furthermore, every source I read through in developing this section stated something along the lines of "hate crimes are dramatically underreported." Therefore, it's possible this is a bigger issue than even the few reputable facts I listed here.

Summary

This very brief overview of the cultural consequences of unchecked fear highlights the trend towards more alienation based upon our differences and more violence, driven by our tribalistic instincts, which seem to be slowly spiraling out of control. Again, some of the trends about hate crime and violence appear to be decreasing, which seems promising. The scary thing is that the general trend for the phenomenon highlighted above essentially shows a slow and steady increase since the mid 90s.

Just as a quick recap, the order of operations goes like this: individual fear consequences lead to more fear in our groups, which leads to rigid group identification (i.e., tribalism), which leads to more intergroup conflict and violence. From sectarian violence in the Middle East to a blossoming of terrorist attacks around the globe in 2016 and 2017, we are so afraid of each other that we've allowed our more repugnant and primal group behaviors to overtake our desire to connect.

To be perfectly clear, I am in no way advocating for an abandoning of culture or group identification. I simply want to highlight how our fear is driving us to over-identify with, and make bad decisions based upon, what "our tribe" says we should do. So, what does this mean on a global scale? As Lao Tzu said, "Violence, even well intentioned, always rebounds on itself."

REFERENCES

1.   Merriam-Webster. (2017). Tribalism. Retrieved on March 22nd, 2017 from: https://www. merriam-webster.com/dictionary/tribalism

2.   Oxford Living Dictionaries (2017). Tribalism. Retrieved on March 22nd, 2017 from: https:// en.oxforddictionaries.com/definition/tribalism

3.   Jenks, C. (1998). *Core Sociological Dichotomies*. SAGE Publications. p. 339. ISBN 978-1-4462-6463-8.

4.   Pievani, T. (2014). Individuals and Groups in Evolution: Darwinian Pluralism and the Multilevel Selection Debate. *Journal of Biosciences*, *39*(2), 319-25. doi:http://dx.doi.org.tcsedsystem.idm.oclc. org/10.1007/s12038-013-9345-4

5.   Dawkins, R. (1989). *The Selfish Gene*. Oxford: Oxford University Press.

6.   Janis, I.L. (1971). Groupthink. *Psychology Today*, *5*, 84-90.

7.   Haselton, M. G., Nettle, D., & Murray, D. R. (2005). *The Evolution of Cognitive Bias. The Handbook of Evolutionary Psychology*.

8.   Whitnall, A. (2016). Global Peace Index 2016: There are Now Only 10 Countries in the World that are Actually Free From Conflict. *Independent*. Retrieved on April 16th, 2017 from: http:// www.independent.co.uk/news/world/politics/global-peace-index-2016-there-are-now-only-10-countries-in-the-world-that-are-not-at-war-a7069816.html

9.   Pettersson, T. & Wallensteen P. (2015). Armed conflicts, 1946–2014. *Journal of Peace Research 4*(52), 536-550.

10.   Pew Research Center (2016). *Discrimination and Conflicts in U.S. Society*. Retrieved on April 12th, 2016 from: http://www.people-press.org/2016/12/08/2-discrimination-and-conflicts-in-u-s-society

11.   Carmichael, R. (2017). Culture Wars: Trap Music Keeps Atlanta on Hip-Hop's Cutting Edge. Why can't the city embrace it? *National Public Radio*. Retrieved on April 10th, 2017 from: http:// www.npr.org/sections/therecord/2017/03/15/520133445/culture-wars-trap-innovation-atlanta-hip-hop

12.   Lowry, R. (2017). Donald Trump's New Culture War. *National Review*. Retrieved on April 10th, 2017 from: http://www.nationalreview.com/article/444156/donald-trump-culture-war

13.   Prothero, S. (2016). Why conservatives start culture wars and liberals win them. *The Washington Post*. Retrieved on April 10th, 2017 from: https://www.washingtonpost.com/opinions/why-conservatives-start-culture-wars-and-liberals-win-them/2016/01/29/f89d0b2c-b658-11e5-a842-0feb51d1d124_story.html?utm_term=.41888aae8f29

14.   Ball, M. (2015). Liberals are Losing the Culture Wars. *The Atlantic*. Retrieved on April 10th, 2017 from:https://www.theatlantic.com/politics/archive/2015/11/liberals-are-losing-the-culture-war/414175/

15.   Salam, R. (2016). Republicans Need a New Approach to Immigration. *National Review*. Retrieved on
      April 10th, 2017 from: http://www.nationalreview.com/article/429192/immigration-new-culture-
      war

16.   Brooks, D. (2016). Let's Have a Better Culture War. *The New York Times*. Retrieved on April 10th,
      2017 from: https://www.nytimes.com/2016/06/07/opinion/lets-have-a-better-culture-war.html?_
      r=0

17.   *The Huffington Post*. (2017). News Categories: Culture wars. Retrieved from: http://www.
      huffingtonpost.com/news/culture-wars/

18.   Snyder, J.A. (2015). America Will Never Move Beyond the Culture Wars. *The New Republic*. Retrieved
      on April 10th, 2017 from: https://newrepublic.com/article/121627/war-soul-america-history-
      culture-wars-review

19.   National Consortium for the Study of Terrorism and Responses to Terrorism (START). (2016).
      Global Terrorism Database [Data file]. Retrieved from https://www.start.umd.edu/gtd

20.   Institute of Race Relations (2017). Racial violence statistics. Retrieved on April 11th, 2017 from:
      http://www.irr.org.uk/research/statistics/racial-violence/

21.   Potok, M. (2015). The Year in Hate and Extremism: Hate and Antigovernment 'Patriot' Groups
      are Down by About a Fifth as Activism Shifts to Cyberspace and Lone Wolf Actions. Southern
      Poverty Law Center. Retrieved on April 11th, 2017 from: https://www.splcenter.org/fighting-hate/
      intelligence-report/2015/year-hate-and-extremism-0

22.   Federal Bureau of Investigations. (2016). Latest hate crime statistics released: Annual report sheds
      light on serious issue. Retrieved on April 11th, 2017 from: https://www.fbi.gov/news/stories/2015-
      hate-crime-statistics-released

"Violence is the last refuge of the incompetent."

ISAAC ASIMOV

CHAPTER 6:
CONSEQUENCS TO WORLD RELATIONS

The consequences discussed so far are born out of our hijacked fear phenomenon, which blossom forth from the previous levels of analysis. Unfortunately, it seems as if consequences at one level of analysis reciprocally reinforce and even exacerbate the consequences discussed at different levels of personal and societal functioning. Now that I've touched on the predominant consequences to us as individuals and cultures/subcultures, I think the last step is to discuss how our fear problem affects global society.

As I have discussed many times throughout this work, the fact of the matter is now that we're all more connected thanks to technology, travel, and advances in economic development, we are all stuck interacting with each other in some way, shape, or form. The new social expectation thanks to social media and how people have chosen to participate on social media is to interact with people whom, 40 years ago, we never would have even thought about reaching out to or getting to know in any meaningful way.

Global relationships are now more important and more normal—statistically speaking—than in previous generations. It seems as if various global, cultural, and technological shifts in the last 100 years are all pushing societies to function in a more global manner, which means more chances to interact with people different from ourselves, participate in fear-inducing dynamics, and become emotionally and cognitively hijacked by social norms.

Whether you believe that we are all part of a global society is not important for the purposes of this discussion. I am not a scholar on international trade or political science, so I'm not intending to step outside my scope and advocate for ideas that I have no basis for supporting given my studies or training. This is not a discussion on the pros and cons of nationalism versus globalism. I could not care less if you prefer a nationalist approach over a globalist one to international and national affairs.

To my knowledge, those concepts are not grounded in any kind of scientific or theoretical academic work about how to best handle geopolitical differences and challenges based upon what we know about human behavior. It would take hundreds of pages to adequately discuss the various ins and outs of geopolitical struggles and make a more definitive statement about how to better approach that topic based upon research in disciplines like psychology, anthropology, or evolutionary biology/psychology as opposed to those that are more superficial (i.e., using a "meta" perspective). But, I don't care, and the topic isn't germane to our fear discussion.

What does matter are the consequences of our fear-based dynamics arising out of geopolitical issues, religion, economics, and wars. I believe there are two consequences arising from our fear problem at the individual and cultural level now manifesting at the global level: global trust issues and more rapid global dynamic changes.

Loss of Trust

The first and deceptively simple consequence of hijacked fear from our individual lives pervading our cultural dynamics is a decrease in our ability to trust our own nations and other nations. Trust is the foundation of most facets of our lives at the individual, cultural, and global levels (1-7). Even the secretary general of the United Nations agrees that we have a global trust problem that's keeping us from solving our problems

(8), which has been echoed by others at the World Economic Forum (9).

This mistrust phenomenon disseminating from global politics and global economic issues has become such a well-known problem that it has become a focus of news headlines (10, 11). A global survey completed last year showed that 57 percent of people distrust foreign governments and 51 percent distrust their own government (12). To be fair, this is only one survey from one group. However, a Pew Research poll from 2015 showed the citizens' trust of the U.S. government at a historic low since 1958 (13), which is somewhat reinforced by Gallup poll numbers (14).

I wonder if these trends would be similar across other industrialized nations? My guess is yes, of course. To be clear, I am not regarding any of the statistics or articles cited above to reflect my personal views or the perfect picture of the world as it is. I only wish to present a snapshot from a few sources of just how prevalent the distrust phenomenon really is in our zeitgeist.

Thinking back to the four drivers of our fear hijacking problem from chapter 3, there are multiple global changes resulting out of our fear—mediated by those four drivers—that have occurred leading to less trust in our own nations and in our allies/enemies. For example, because of the incredible changes in technology, we can rapidly communicate, engage in military actions, and research each other (i.e., spy on) with extreme ease.

Now, spying on our neighbors has been going on since the times of Sun Tzu and Julius Caesar (15), but the pace and scope of spying has rapidly grown in the last 50 years. There is something like over 1,300 satellites in earth's orbit (16). In the U.S. alone, there are 1,200-plus government groups and almost 2,000 private businesses working on intelligence and security issues (17). Taking just these two facts, think about how much access we have for keeping tabs on each other at home and abroad.

An article a few years ago found that the NSA alone was responsible for over 2,000 erroneous spying incidents in 2012 (18). If there are thousands of erroneous spying incidents in one year, it's safe to extrapolate and assume there are at least tens of thousands, if not hundreds of thousands, of sanctioned spying incidents in a year. Combine these numbers with the leaked information provided by Edward Snowden in 2013, and it's a fair bet to say that other world powers are built and operate in a similar fashion.

For some reason, industrialized nations feel a strong need to invest excessive amounts of time, money, and other resources into intelligence-gathering. Well, there are many variables that go into our desire to keep tabs on each other, but the simple explanation is, we are highly suspect of each other (i.e., fear).

A second example of fear about espionage relating to the U.S. was our 2016 presidential election. On both sides of the major campaigns during the election, and for almost the entirety of the first six months of 2017, there have been so many rumors, stories, and "leaks" related to espionage efforts within the U.S. and from other major world powers relating to candidate Hillary Clinton and President Donald Trump.

The international community is in such a state of distrust that it has now seeped into presidential elections around the world. Now, to be fair, major world powers have been engaging in spying and espionage efforts since the early 1900s, and I'm certain historical versions of our modern world powers engaged in spying behavior as well (15).

Our distrust (i.e., fear) of our neighbors and our own citizens has been able to flourish thanks to the technological explosion of the last 100 years. As noted earlier, trust is a fundamental aspect of human behavior across most domains of our lives. I believe it is important that we engage in a reality check about just how mistrusting the global scene has become. Mistrust not only leads to expenditures of energy and finances, but also to serious conflicts.

Global Dynamics on Hyper Drive

The second consequence I believe that has arisen out of our inability to have a healthy relationship with our fear process is a dramatic increase in the pace of global dynamics. I believe the rapid pace of global relationships and economic/military dynamics results in only more stress or more fear for all parties involved.

It's a safe assumption that we feel the need to relate to each other in a much more impulsive manner thanks to the last 40 years of advances in communication technology, military technology, and increased commerce between industrialized/non-industrialized nations (19). Of course, it is only fair to say that none of these advances and changes represent an inherently or completely harmful process.

I do, however, wish to argue that the quicker we act and react with each other on the international stage, the more likely it is that bad decisions are going to be made and more unnecessary civil/emotional/existential distance will be created between nations or other global economic actors. One simple example is the oil trade. Economists have been predicting that the increase in population, changes in technology, and changes in global economics will slow oil consumption down due to reported availability of crude oil. The most recent analysis shows that the upswing in demand for oil has shifted consumer/national behavior towards an even more rapid consumption and growth pace (20-21), which is similar for other facets of global trade as more countries enter the trading arena (22, 23). This might even be affecting the environment and how animal species function (24).

Technological development and implementation is now moving and growing faster than the legal system can keep up with in countries like the U.S. (25, 26). All of this rapid growth leads to more fear about things like the availability of resources, stability of companies, and stability of national relationships or corporate relationships. This results in more conflict in negotiating international politics and legal policies as well (27).

Here's another simple example that might illuminate my point somewhat more directly and concretely. Let's try another thought experiment about just how fast life moves nowadays thanks to communication technology. Imagine, if you will, life 80 years ago, right around 1937. Jonas Salk had not yet created the Polio vaccine, and many were still suffering and dying from preventable diseases. World War II had not yet begun. The Hindenburg Disaster occurred. It was the Great Depression era. There was no internet and no advanced communication technology apart from the telegram, which was popular but sparsely available. Shipping of mail messages about any local or international affairs mentioned above would take many days because the mail was delivered via train (28) and something like only 40 percent of households had telephones at the time (29).

This likely meant that if someone wanted to communicate with you, we would have to wait a significant amount of time to hear or read the message being sent. Can you imagine waiting three to five days to get a message from a loved one or a coworker in a different city? Or for mail being shipped overseas about how finance and wars are progressing in other parts of the world? This meant that businesses moved slower, relationships formed more slowly, and people had to be patient in trying to understand what was happening in the world. This likely meant slow growth in global trade, more time was needed for countries to get involved in global military conflicts, or that simple communications about international politics occurred over the course of many hours, or even days.

Fast-forward to 2017. The great majority of people have phones in their homes/office (29), if not cell phones, as well as email messaging. These forms of communication are instantaneous. We hear of an outbreak of a new form of the flu virus or a global conflict and we can all know within a matter of mere minutes, if not seconds, that something has happened.

Given that we have the capacity to learn about events and communicate with each other so much more rapidly, it stands to reason that our global leaders now are making decisions about important issues much more quickly than in the past.

As discussed earlier, this likely has a significant impact on global politics, economics, military conflict, and every other important aspect of global interaction. Given the advancements in military, nautical, and aeronautics technologies, we can strike back or preemptively act in military conflicts in a few hours, compared to the old technology of the 1930s. Common fighter jets of the 1930s, like the "Bristol Blenheim" Royal Air Force fighter, for example, flew at speeds of about 200 to 300 miles per hour, whereas the fastest jets of the modern day, like the SR-71 Blackbird or the Russian MIG, fly at over 2,200 miles per hour.

If we take a serious look at just how dramatically technology has changed, and how much more capably and rapidly we can move and communicate, then our world influencers must be making global decisions based upon an understanding that we can impact other societies very easily and quickly.

I hypothesize that our almost instantaneous ability to affect each other across the world must have some sort of impact on how afraid we are of each other on the global stage. This leads me to my final point of this chapter and of this entire treatise on how our unchecked fear problem is working and growing towards a dangerous way of being for everyone on the planet.

A Final Concern

C ombine the rapid global dynamic change with the distrust discussed above, and I think we have a very concerning state of global affairs that deserves some discussion. When I started this book, my goal was to help people understand just how unaware they are of their fear process and how it impacts their life in a very concrete and immediate manner. Since diving into the research process and refining my theories with colleagues, I've found that our unchecked fear issue is not a simple problem with an easy solution.

The reality is, because of the incredible advances in economics and technology, our current global conflicts about trade, religion, and politics can now be a great impediment to human progress. These advancements could also result in life-ending wars using nuclear technology and bio-weapons, which have become remarkably well-understood and simpler to engineer (30).

The importance of cultures/nations adequately understanding the complexities of international affairs cannot be understated, simply because the less informed we are, the more we engage in groupthink and develop a fear-based perspective about others—discussed in the previous chapter (31). The sad reality is that major world powers like the U.S. (and most other countries) are struggling to trust each other because of corruption and ideological disparities (32, 24). I believe we all have arrived at a time in history with sufficient access to knowledge and capability to steer the ship out of harm's way but are choosing not to do so in an appropriate or consistent manner.

To drive this point home and wrap up this multi-chapter exploration of our individual-cultural-global fear problem, let's just do some math together to prove how threatening our circumstances really are. Please keep in mind I'm speaking from the perspective of someone living in the U.S. Moreover, this is a thought experiment about which I cannot say definitively that a person will always be afraid of the things I will list off below.

On an individual level, there are a number of daily experiences that will typically cause us to have fear: possibly being hit while driving, being on time to appointments, finding a job/maintaining employment, deciding about education, checking social media, watching the news, discussing politics, finding food, maintaining relationships, raising families, managing finances, paying off debts, government corruption (35), wondering if our doctors are trustworthy (36), advancing in society, and figuring out the meaning of life.

At the cultural level people often struggle with (i.e., feel afraid of) people of different race, ethnicity, gender, sexuality, religion, political ideology, educational level, type of profession, and level of social standing daily. At the global level, again, speaking from the perspective of someone living in the U.S., it's common nowadays to feel fear about the status of wars in the Middle East, possible (and likely) spread of Islamic extremism, Russia, China, North Korea, global trade/economic issues, environmental disasters, and global warming. This list could also contain many more fear experiences of varying degrees of intensity depending upon your life circumstances. To be fair, not every person has their life setup in a stereotypical Western fashion.

Adding these ideas and situations up, there are a total of at least 33 circumstances to feel fear about every day. Let's focus on just one of the examples above and estimate the number of times we have a fear response when engaged with something like, say, watching the news about politics. Given the repetitive and sensationalist nature of news media in the U.S., it would be fair to estimate that the average person will have a fear response at least a half dozen times in just one hour about politics.

It's a fair estimation, I assert, that we have hundreds of fear reactions occurring in our brains in a day while relating to people, working, consuming news media or social media, and going about our daily lives in the Western world. With all these daily fear experiences, it's no small wonder that we argue so often and have such conflict the world over.

This makes me *fear* that things are insidiously getting out of control, and I believe I've made a clear case to support my assertion. Now that there is a clear understanding of the state of fear in the world, I want to spend a moment with you discussing what I believe our future could look like. Obviously, there are billions of variables to consider when pondering the world and predicting the future.

It is difficult to speculate about specific future occurrences in any meaningful way, which is outside of my scope of practice and the scope of this book anyways. Given all that has been discussed up to this point, I think I can reasonably assume that we are heading in one of two general directions on this planet that will vary to some degree or another.

First, it is altogether likely that we will continue fighting more, engage more often in wars, become more politically partisan, more religiously divided and hostile about our beliefs, more rigidly tribalistic/nationalistic, and could even end up engaging in nuclear war with each other. This scenario is rather scary because, unlike 60 years ago, many more nations and dictators have access to nuclear weapons or the means to create nasty bioweapons.

Despite the U.N. and other international agencies attempting to step in to regulate or prevent others from creating such weapons, so many aspects of the market for dangerous technology and weapons are unregulated, or even simply hidden. Although we do not commonly discuss this, anyone using the dark web and teaming up with rogue scientists adhering to dangerous political and/or religious ideologies could relatively easily create a nuclear weapon or bioweapon and inflict massive amounts of damage on unsuspecting victims. Let us all hope that this is not the case, but it's not difficult to imagine our fear problem continuing to spiral out of control to the point where this happens.

The second possible alternative is more hopeful—though I'm skeptical that this will happen because we are not addressing the underlying fear problems in any meaningful or impactful way. We all become a little more rational and develop a more mindful relationship with our fear instincts. World leaders, individuals, cultures, religious groups, economic powers, and the like all start to wonder *how do we keep this game going long term?*

Slowly and steadily, people discuss the root problem in a more concrete way, avoiding the red herrings of politics, tribalism, religion, and economics as their rationalizations for living in a fear-driven mindset. Individuals, cultures, and nations begin developing more adaptive solutions to conflicts guided by a balance of intellectually-honest reasoning and a healthy adherence to self-preservation born out of our gut feelings.

Please bear in mind that I'm not advocating for a Kumbaya way of living because, as I stated in previous chapters, that is also not quite how we are designed. Humans are much more complicated and part of living in a complicated life is normal and expectable conflict. This alternative is about how we choose to deal with our acute conflicts, our urges, and our existential struggles. Alternative number two could be one of the most ideal and optimistic outcomes for our fear-problem—though unlikely.

As promised at the beginning of this journey, I will devote the final chapter to a discussion of tools, tips, tricks, ideas, and shifts that might help manage this fear problem in a more adaptive way that could lead to alternative number two. Before I end this section, I simply want to impress upon you again how concerning our state of affairs is shaping up to be based upon the logic used in the previous chapters. It is easy to write off parts of my arguments in both reasonable and unreasonable ways.

For example, given how "good" life is in Western or industrialized nations, it is difficult to fully own the idea that something as small as a biased perspective due to our religion, culture, education, or other socializing phenomenon can be problematic enough to result in potential nuclear war. Given the problems of lacking intellectual honesty and faulty coping, the fear associated with our small unchecked biases and other reasonable or unreasonable fears experienced at the individual level begin to congeal and create cultural mindsets of fear-based tribalism, which then leads to international issues.

Human beings and human cultures are complex systems, and I find it difficult to believe that a problem or error at one level of functioning does not affect other aspects of the system. So, please, despite how incredulous some of my ideas or assertions may seem, read on to the last chapter and see if any of the reasoning or tips/tricks/tools could be helpful.

REFERENCES

1.   Michalos, Alex C. "The impact of trust on business, international security and the quality of life." *How Good Policies and Business Ethics Enhance Good Quality of Life*. Springer International Publishing, 2017. 127-153.

2.   Erikson, E. H. (1950). *Childhood and Society.* New York, NY: Norton.

3.   Erikson, E.H. (1963). *Childhood and Society* (2nd Ed.). New York, NY: Norton

4.   Mach, M., & Lvina, E. (2017). When trust in the leader matters: The moderated-mediation model of team performance and trust. *Journal of Applied Sport Psychology, 29*(2), 134-149.

5.   Mitchell, R. M., Ripley, J., Adams, C., & Raju, D. (2011). Trust an Essential Ingredient in Collaborative Decision Making. *Journal of School Public Relations, 32*(2), 145-170.

6.   Boeckmann, R. J., & Tyler, T. R. (2002). Trust, respect, and the psychology of political engagement. *Journal of Applied Social Psychology, 32*(10), 2067-2088.

7.   Evans, A. M., & Krueger, J. I. (2009). The psychology (and economics) of trust. *Social and Personality Psychology Compass, 3*(6), 1003-1017.

8.   Yakupitiyage, T. (2017). Mistrust hindering global solutions, says Secretary General. *Inter Press Service News Agency*. Retrieved on May 1st, 2017 from: http://www.ipsnews.net/2017/02/mistrust-hindering-global-solutions-says-secretary-general/

9.   Griffiths, A. & Costa, N. (2017). Why world mistrust must not threaten the 2030 agenda for sustainable development. *World Economic Forum*. Retrieved on May 3rd, 2017 from: https://www.weforum.org/agenda/2017/01/why-world-mistrust-must-not-threaten-the-2030-agenda-for-sustainable-development/

10. Goodwin, M. (2014). Obama's lies have led to global mistrust. *The New York Post Retrieved* on May 3rd, 2017 from: http://nypost.com/2014/04/23/obamas-lies-have-led-to-global-mistrust/

11. Gonzalez, E. (2017). Trump's world involves global fragility, mercantilism, and mistrust. *The Diplomat in Spain*. Retrieved on May 3rd, 2017 from: http://thediplomatinspain.com/en/trumps-world-involves-global-fragility-mercantilism-and-mistrust/

12. Beard-Knolwand, T. (2017). Brands in the age of mistrust: The search for simplicity and control. *Ipsos Global Trends*. Retrieved on May 1st, 2017 from https://www.ipsosglobaltrends.com/brands-in-the-age-of-mistrust/

13. The Pew Research Center. (2016). *Trust in government: 1958-2015*. Retrieved on June 6th, 2017 from: http://www.people-press.org/2015/11/23/1-trust-in-government-1958-2015/

14. GALLUP. (2017). *Trust in government*. Retrieved on June 6th, 2017 from: http://www.gallup.com/poll/5392/trust-government.aspx

15.   Zurcher, A. (2013). *Roman Empire to the NSA: A world history of government spying*. BBC News, Magazine. Retrieved on May 1st, 2017 from: http://www.bbc.com/news/magazine-24749166

16.   Astronomy Magazine (2017). *New interactive chart shows just how many satellites are orbiting Earth: Just how much future space trash is up there?* Retrieved on May 1st, 2017 from: http://www.astronomy.com/news/2017/01/interactive-satellite-chart

17.   Priest, D. & Arkin, W.M. (2010). A hidden world, growing beyond control. *The Washington Post*. Retrieved on May 1st, 2017 from: http://projects.washingtonpost.com/top-secret-america/articles/a-hidden-world-growing-beyond-control/

18.   Gellman, B. (2013). NSA broke privacy rule thousands of times per year, audit finds. *The Washington Post*. Retrieved on May 1st, 2017 from: https://www.washingtonpost.com/world/national-security/nsa-broke-privacy-rules-thousands-of-times-per-year-audit-finds/2013/08/15/3310e554-05ca-11e3-a07f-49ddc7417125_story.html?utm_term=.f5d894800765

19.   Poscente, V. (2008). *The age of speed: Learning to thrive in a more-faster-now world*. New York, NY: Ballantine Books.

20.   Dargay, J. M., & Gately, D. (2010). World oil demand's shift toward faster growing and less price-responsive products and regions. *Energy Policy, 38*(10), 6261-6277.

21.   Oliver, H. H. (2010). Moving more, faster, and further in a carbon constrained world. *Harvard Asia Quarterly, 12*, 4-14.

22.   Dean, M., & Sebastia-Barriel, M. (2004). Why has world trade grown faster than world output?. *Bank of England*. Quarterly Bulletin, *44*(3), 310-320.

23.   Hanson, G. H. (2012). The Rise of Middle Kingdoms: Emerging Economies in Global Trade. *Journal of Economic Perspectives, 26*(2), 41-64.

24.   Tewksbury, J. J., Sheldon, K. S., & Ettinger, A. K. (2011). *Ecology: Moving farther and faster. Nature Climate Change, 1*(8), 396-397.

25.   Lewis, A. (2014). The legality of 3D printing: how technology is moving faster than the law. *Tulane Journal of Technology & Intellectual Property, 17*, 303-317.

26.   Kerry, K. (2001). *Music on the Internet: Is Technology Moving Faster Than Copyright Law*. Santa Clara Law Review., *42*, 967-993.

27.   Stone, D. (2008). Global public policy, transnational policy communities, and their networks. *Policy Studies Journal, 36*(1), 19-38.

28.   Smithsonian National Postal Museum (2017). *History of the service: Decades of change 1920s-1950s*. Retrieved on May 1st, 2017 from: https://postalmuseum.si.edu/rms/history/decades.html

29.   Statista. (2017). Percentage of housing units with telephones in the United States from 1920 to 2008. Retrieved on May 1st, 2017 from: https://www.statista.com/statistics/189959/housing-units-with-telephones-in-the-united-states-since-1920/

30.   Foley, M. (2013). Genetically engineered bioweapons: A new breed of weapons for modern warfare. *Dartmouth Undergraduate Journal of Science*. Retrieved on July 21st, 2017 from: http://dujs.dartmouth.edu/2013/03/genetically-engineered-bioweapons-a-new-breed-of-weapons-for-

modern-warfare/#.WXPsDf_yuRs

31.   Brewer, P. R., Gross, K., Aday, S., & Willnat, L. (2004). International trust and public opinion about world affairs. *American Journal of Political Science, 48*(1), 93-109.

32.   Kydd, A. H. (2005). Trust and mistrust in international relations. *Princeton University Press.*

33.   Brewer, P. R., Aday, S., & Gross, K. (2005). Do Americans trust other nations? A panel study. *Social Science Quarterly, 86*(1), 36-51.

34.   Torgler, B. (2008). Trust in international organizations: An empirical investigation focusing on the United Nations. *The Review of International Organizations, 3*(1), 65-93.

35.   Bowerman, M. (2016). Survey reveals what Americans fear most. USA Today Network. Retrieved on July 21st, 2017 from: https://www.usatoday.com/story/news/nation-now/2016/10/12/survey-top-10-things-americans-fear-most/91934874/

36.   Blendon, R. J., Benson, J. M., & Hero, J. O. (2014). Public trust in physicians—US medicine in international perspective. *New England Journal of Medicine, 371*(17), 1570-1572.

> "Progress is impossible without change,
> and those who cannot change their minds
> cannot change anything."
>
> GEORGE BERNARD SHAW

CHAPTER 7:
SOLUTIONS FOR ATTENUATING FEAR

A Call for Change

Well, here we are at the end of this fear problem journey. I want to start off by saying that although some of the facts, assertions, and arguments are admittedly discussed in an alarmist tone, the goal is not to incite more unnecessary fear or cause a state of panic for those of you reading. My hope has been to illuminate ideas and argue in a manner that is evocative enough to push us to change. I say "us" because I am no different: no better, no worse. I fall into the same fear traps and engage in the same problematic dynamics.

Given the challenges discussed up to this point, it seems clear to me, at least, that much needs to be done to right the ship and counteract the fear problem adequately. The enormity, insidiousness, and complexity of the fear problem is why I believe we need to all take some responsibility for the state of affairs and put energy towards new or overlooked solutions.

As for my part in helping combat the fear problem, I have some thoughts to share about how we can work on an individual, cultural, and global level to move towards a more balanced and mindful relationship with fear. Furthermore, while I do not believe it will magically disappear, we can start shifting towards a less fear-oriented way of living, more in line with how we're naturally designed to function.

First, I believe an individual approach is necessary for avoiding the foreseeable negative consequences of the fear problem. In fact, I argue that the most fundamental means of improving the fear problem is at the individual level because, obviously, cultures and global societies are merely groups of individuals. As I referenced with the Shaw quote on the previous page, I think the main goal for the individual approach to remediating the fear problem is a shifting of mindsets and attitudes. I will offer well-reasoned and scientifically-supported fear management practices to that end.

Secondarily, I believe that there are some practicable strategies to implement at the cultural level that do not upend philosophies and customs or destroy what most cultures hold dear to make members of said culture feel accepted. I do not believe we need to destroy cultures, simply help them evolve through effort as members of our various cultural groups.

Finally, I propose that the powers controlling or influencing decisions on a global level can engage in specific activities and mindset shifts to help improve our fear problem, and even prevent more catastrophic consequences from occurring. Just as the consequences of the fear problem all build upon each other, I believe that these strategies for remediating the fear problem can also come together in a positive direction.

Again, I have no misgivings about how illogical it is to strive for a one world society or an idyllic Kumbaya sense of brotherhood. This will hopefully serve as a more rational discussion about how we can all, me included, manage the unending and seemingly intractable struggles of existence and relationships.

Individual Strategies

W e need to have a personal investment in change and a willingness to live a healthier lifestyle to combat the fear problem at an individual level. I propose we all do our part individually, and if we're part of highly reactive cultures, encourage a more mindful dialogue and a stance of thoughtful activism (as opposed to reactionary activism). I discussed the two consequences to ourselves as individuals in chapter 4 (i.e., loss of intellectual honesty and maladaptive coping), and I believe we need to focus on reversing those consequences.

In that spirit, I propose strategies that either promote more intellectual honesty or simply help us cope more adaptively (i.e., have a more mindful and balanced relationship with our fear process). Specifically, I want to focus on how to incorporate what many authors and researchers describe as a lifestyle of "wellness." I'm going to borrow my definition of wellness from Dan Siegel, a brilliant author in the psychology and psychiatry world.

A lifestyle of wellness, according to Dr. Siegel and Dr. David Rock, is an "integrated" sense of wellbeing or fulfillment built on the pillars of healthy sleep, physical activity, play, focus (i.e., critical thinking) time, intimate connections, relaxation, and "time in" (i.e., meditation or self-attunement) (1). The link to their helpful website is listed in the resources section at the end of this chapter.

Although all the wellness concepts discussed above can work in concert to help us address our individual fear hijacking process, I want to focus on "time in" so that we can not only cope better but also relate and think in a more intellectually honest manner. Please, look up the other concepts and check out the resources at the end to see how you can create a lifestyle of wellness by getting better sleep, eating better, being active appropriately, keeping your mind engaged, and staying connected.

The wellness concept Dr. Siegel supports is based upon the most integrated neuroscientific understanding of human mind-relationship-health functioning. To have a healthier sense of "time in," I want to propose three specific strategies: mindfulness meditation, a self "check-up," and a strategic conflict resolution technique to de-escalate interpersonal conflict, which I describe with the acronym P.A.S.T.A.

Mindfulness

Perhaps the most underutilized tool for managing our emotional states, outside of exercise, is mindfulness. This practice, which is thousands of years old, has had some popularity in the last 20 or so years. Although mindfulness is typically associated with Eastern cultures and religions, I want to discuss it from the brain/body perspective.

From the last 40 years of research within the fields of medicine and psychology, it is reasonable to assert that maybe a little bit of quiet time focused on our breathing can be of great benefit to stopping the fear hijacking process at the individual level of functioning. Mindfulness meditation promotes attentional focus and lessening of anxiety-induced distraction (2). Moreover, mindfulness meditation is commonly accepted as a method for managing anxiety across a variety of situations (3-10).

Research over the past 20 years has shown that mindfulness-based practices are so effective for managing fear/anxiety because meditations of this nature increase activation of frontal/relational brain areas responsible for affect regulation, as I discussed in chapter 2 (11). Essentially, using mindfulness practices allows us to have less anxiety, a greater ability to focus, and a greater likelihood of responding with fewer or less intense judgments.

I believe we need to engage in a more mindful approach towards ourselves and those around us because our hijacked brain-fear problem is not simply a problem for ourselves. A growing trend in trauma/anxiety research is focused on intergenerational transmission and epigenetics.

The standing theory in the field of epigenetics of mental health nowadays is that some of our genetic profile for being sensitive to traumatic experiences (i.e., our ability to feel "overwhelmed" or hijacked) is passed down genetically for generations (12-16). Moreover, addiction, as a predominant means of coping discussed earlier in chapter 4, also has a genetic component (17), so it would be good if we didn't pass on any predispositions.

As a caveat, some of these genetic predisposition studies have come under question. However, the general conversation in the field is pointing towards support for attempting to understand how our life experiences shape our brain, which shapes our genes, which can be passed onto the next generation. If other mental health conditions like bipolar disorder, psychosis, and major depression have a genetic component, it's not unreasonable to think our fear sensitivity can have a genetic basis.

The goal here is to engage in relationships with ourselves and others in such a way that we can live more *realistically* trusting, and with less fear of each other. Trust is very important because it allows us to work together adaptively. Also, it feels good, releasing endogenous oxytocin (18). The more mindful we are, the easier it will be to form accurate (i.e., unbiased) judgments about others and feel safer and more connected.

Utilizing a mindfulness technique on a regular basis should help greatly in the fight against both intellectual dishonesty as well as maladaptive coping. If we can develop a regular mindfulness routine, our daily experiences of anxiety should decrease. This means we theoretically can think more clearly to promote more intellectually honest conversation and intellectually honest self-examination. Furthermore, if we feel more consistently calm and centered, for which mindfulness practice is designed, then we're less likely to want to check out using drugs, alcohol, social media, sex, excessive exercise, and the like (19-21).

The goal here is not for radical change. I have no desire for everyone to become Buddhist monks or yogis. The goal is just to encourage you to engage in a new exercise promoting greater mind-body awareness, which calms you down and allows you to think more clearly. Meditation is by no means a cure-all, simply a nice adjunctive tool to help all people— including myself—manage the all-too-frequent anxieties and fears we experience. The next tool, the "self check-in," will promote even greater capacity for intellectual honesty so that we can check our biases, judgments, and other facets of ignorance and hypocrisy that fester in our minds every day.

Self Check-In

One of the issues I outlined in the section on intellectual honesty in chapter 4 is how people often automatically react or engage in biased thinking. To tackle our biases and our more automatic responding way of being, we need to—metaphorically—shove a stick in the spokes of our mental wheels to get back to a realistic and intellectually honest manner of thinking.

To be frank, I think we all need to re-learn how to operate more pragmatically, so I'm going to borrow from the comedian Craig Ferguson as a simple example of the process I believe is badly needed to rectify this intellectual honesty problem. In one of his shows, Mr. Ferguson talks about his history of failed marriages, alcoholism, and interpersonal conflicts. Finally, he relays to the audience that he has begun asking himself three questions: "Does this need to be said?" and "Does this need to be said by me?" "Does this need to be said by me, now?"

Although his standup routine is designed for getting a laugh from his audiences by telling hyperbolic stories, the gravitas in his three questions is quite apparent given the discussion of his prior relationships and life chaos. The principle underlying Mr. Ferguson's three questions is how to self-monitor, or check-in with oneself before engaging in interpersonal stupidity. To successfully achieve this reality check like Craig Ferguson's three questions, I want to combine a few concepts into one to describe our self check-in technique.

We need a new habit; we need to return to our "kernel of intellectual honesty" as Guenin described it (22). So, I'm going to propose a tripartite check-in process that anyone can simply, but not easily, implement into their daily routine. I want to differentiate "simple" from "easy" for you because I do not wish to mislead you about the challenge that lies ahead of you if you so choose to follow through with this technique.

What I'm about to recommend is clear, makes sense, and has few moving parts/concepts, which makes it simple. The problem is that because of our already hijacked brains, we will have to use great mental effort to fully undertake this new exercise and essentially retrain our brains and fight our evolutionary programming.

Again, this fear problem is the result of our healthy or evolutionarily adaptive fear response to perceived rejection or threats to safety having been "wired" (i.e., conditioned) to respond to ideas, concepts, and experiences that are neither imminently threatening nor important. As part of the rewiring process, hopefully in conjunction with some daily mindfulness meditations, I think the first part of the tripartite model should be a tool for challenging our notions prior to any fear response occurring. The simplest and most powerful tool for challenging our assumptions is a technique that is hundreds of years old and more recently incorporated into psychology/psychotherapy practices called *Socratic questioning*.

Although it would be helpful to become acquainted with Socrates, (his life, his rationale for developing a logic system, etc.), I will leave that for you to explore on your own. In the resources section at the end of the book, I have listed some good reads on Socrates and his logic system. Socratic questioning is a quick and dirty method for getting to the bottom of an assumption, idea, or belief. Literally, the goal of this exercise is to help you challenge your own suppositions using your own knowledge of both "common sense" and consequences.

There are many versions of Socratic questioning exercises, but they all boil down to a few basic types of questions: clarification of ideas, foundation exploration, showing counter-evidence, perspective challenges, and evidentiary expansion. To streamline this to be a simple step in our tripartite model, I'm going to leave you with four questions you should ask yourself *every time* you find yourself thinking about any topic that has been, is, or could be a source of contention.

- How clear (i.e., detailed or nuanced) is my belief/perspective?
- What facts—not life experiences—support my belief/perspective?
- Have I considered all facts that both support and challenge my belief/perspective?
- Have I fully considered my biases and their influence on my belief/perspective?

These questions are, as I promised, very simple. I recommend performing this exercise often, if not daily then at least on a weekly basis. This exercise is designed to be carried out in your free time, not during an argument. If your answer to any of these questions is "I'm not sure," then more thought and reflection is needed before asserting your opinion. If your answer to the fourth question is "No," then I implore you to do yourself and others the kindness of questioning your biases.

Our emotional history and life experiences greatly shape our biases, and many of the stupid and needless arguments that occur on the news, at the bar, at the dinner table, in congress, and, frankly, anywhere typically arise from unchecked biases leading to emotional hijacking. Your life experiences are/were real, but they're not facts and cannot serve as verifiable evidence of a phenomenon being either useful or maladaptive.

Life experiences hold no weight, and should carry no weight, when talking about concepts like how to better manage taxes, politics, economics, medicine, biology, prejudice, discrimination, or any other important subject. We need to be more mindful of the statistics and develop realistic predictions about the future—the rate of change as it were—like in the example I used in chapter 3 about the state and rate of LGBTQIA progress in the United States.

The second part of our tripartite model for restoring intellectual honesty is deceptively simple: avoid asserting your opinion regarding topics about which you do not know the facts. To be clear, I'm not advocating for some kind of draconian free speech suppression. I'm harkening back to the Craig Ferguson method of avoiding interpersonal drama.

If we don't really know what we're talking about, and typically we get in arguments about topics that we haven't fully explored, then why set yourself up for a waste of time arguing? I fully support you asking questions—in a non-accusatory tone—about ideas or concepts about which you have an opinion. In fact, if you find yourself faced with someone espousing ideas with which you disagree, ask the four Socratic questions listed above in a non-threatening manner. Even if that argument gets heated, you successfully challenged not only your own thought process, but also another's point of view, which is a gigantic leap in the right direction.

This is perhaps the most difficult component of the tripartite model because it seems as if we all, myself included, are almost habitually inclined to jump right into an argument nowadays. The level of discourse in many Western countries, with the U.S. being perhaps the saddest example, has fallen to the low of constant argument sans critical thought.

We need to break this habit, and we need to break this habit quickly so that we can reacquire a sense of basic human decency in our discourse. For example, how many of you in the U.S. and abroad have said ridiculous things in arguments and even broken ties with people over something relating to politics or President Donald Trump?

I highly encourage you to stop right now and just think to yourself. Consider the wide array of topics that you have argued about and how much you actually know about the topics. These are the topics to avoid until more critical thought and more effort has been put forth into a fuller understanding. This fruitless behavior needs to stop.

The final part of our tripartite model for bolstering intellectual honesty is also deceptively simple. I encourage you to force yourself to spend 30 minutes per week listening to a contrasting viewpoint about any topic that you believe is important. This applies to fact-driven concepts like scientific phenomena, politics, economics, and health.

I also highly encourage some direct challenging of more philosophical and fluid topics like your religious beliefs, values, and the various aspects of your sense of self. This may seem like it fits within the first segment of the tripartite model, but it's an activity that needs emphasis in our goal of rebuilding a mindset of intellectual honesty.

The nice thing about engaging in a structured activity devoted to learning new perspectives is that we only gain by functioning in this way. The worst thing that can happen by devoting time to new perspectives is you lose some time out of your day to someone preaching absolute nonsense. This can only help support a more intellectually honest point of view because now you've fully processed one counterargument.

What is most important in this exercise is, again, like I referenced in the introduction and later chapters, attempting to listen with an attitude of transformative learning. The more reasonably open-minded we are about listening to people speak, the more likely it is that we gain knowledge to bolster an argument or use the ideas we disagree with to refine our own arguments.

To review, the tripartite model for rebuilding a mindset of intellectual honesty is composed of the four Socratic questions, healthy avoidance of superficially understood topics, and 30 minutes of challenging your views. I hope these tripartite model tools are clear and my reasoning makes sense to you.

The potential pros of engaging in this tripartite exercise could include the following: less time wasted arguing, more peace of mind, a more flexible mindset, a greater fund of knowledge about important topics, fewer reasons to "check out" in relationships/because of relationships and forming better relationships.

The potential consequences of engaging in this tripartite exercise are: 30 minutes lost per week challenging yourself, a period of cognitive dissonance about your long-held beliefs or opinions, and wanting an apology from or feeling compelled to apologize to others with whom we've argued. To help with the relational aspect of promoting change at the individual level of functioning, my final tool should serve as a starting point for repairing or improving the quality of relationships as a means of feeling less afraid and more emotionally safe.

P.A.S.T.A.

My little acronym, P.A.S.T.A., is a quick de-escalation trick for when we're starting to feel "heated" with each other or when things are already at a problematic level of discourse—or maybe even just arguing/ fighting. It stands for *Pause, Acknowledge, Separate, Try again,* and *Apologize.*

Simple enough, right? The goal for this tool is simply to start breaking the chain of needless arguments in which we all engage on a rather frequent basis, especially here in the U.S. You've likely heard of similar conflict de-escalation techniques, and I hope that my variation is simple and effective. This is a tool I have used with clients, families, friends, and strangers that seems to manage the here and now in a more productive manner when things are getting heated.

The first step is pause. To pause appropriately, I recommend between 15-30 seconds of you not responding to the other person in the situation that is starting to become heated. This might feel awkward and unfamiliar, and it should. The majority of us were never taught to cool off when we feel activated. Just sit with the awkwardness of the silence so that your brain, particularly your frontal cortex, can begin to do its job to help your midbrain calm down and start processing things more logically.

The second step is to acknowledge, specifically acknowledge that you feel hijacked or heated and that you do not wish for things to get worse. This is about you, not the other person. Research shows that by actively stating what we have experienced (i.e., verbalizing and externalizing feelings) we feel a slight sense of anxiety relief (23, 24). Interestingly, some brain research shows that verbalizing our problems in a mindful manner helps decrease the tension in the moment (25).

Essentially, by using our critical thinking parts of the brain responsible for language, awareness, and analysis (i.e., pre-frontal lobes areas), it decreases the activity of our more emotional and reactive parts of the brain (i.e., the amygdala). Moreover, due to feeling less tense by verbalizing our problems, which begins to decrease our interpersonal tension, it reinforces our healthy *sense of agency* (26), our belief in our ability to effectively manage our lives.

Another way of looking at this acknowledgment idea is to think of it as a first attempt at being healthily assertive amidst a stressful situation. Indeed, assertiveness is a major positive force in the resolution of conflicts (27). If you find yourself separating for a longer period, it might be wise to engage in the Socratic questioning component of the self check-in discussed above.

The third step is to separate. I recommend at least five minutes of space when we feel like we're about to get heated with each other, and longer if we are already mid argument. From a basic neuroscience perspective, when we get *hijacked*—to whatever degree—our emotional midbrain centers literally are so overactivated that our higher up, frontal skills are shut down and need to be very intentionally brought back online. Ergo, if you have successfully completed the acknowledgment step correctly (given the circumstances), you have already lessened both of your emotional storms by using your frontal cortex powers to name and have a modicum of mastery over your immediate emotional states.

This process sets the stage, or primes the brain, for continued frontal cortex control over the emotional centers (i.e., amygdala, etc.) of your midbrain (11). Again, I'm not proposing we "think" our way into having control over our feelings, because that's literally impossible—despite what cognitive therapists may say! I am, however, proposing that we have a more neurologically integrated way of processing and coping with our feelings—á la Dan Siegel's goal of an integrated mind, a key strategy for both living well and mental health (28).

In this way, asking to separate is an active frontal cortex process that involves reasoning, planning, and memory, increases our frontal cortex functioning, and balances out our emotional state while adding some mental free space to breathe. This space to breathe can further decrease the intensity of our emotional states in pretty much any setting and with most emotional struggles (11, 29, 30).

Finally, after separating for a substantial period, the goal is to try the conversation again. If it appears like you or the other person in your midst is still in an emotionally hijacked state, then it would be wise to cool down some more and go back to separating. If you both appear relatively calm, then it is worth trying to articulate your feelings and beliefs again in as non-aggressive and intellectually honest a manner as you can muster.

If things were already in a heated argument prior to pausing, this might also be a good time to apologize. The goal of this step is simply keeping the conversation and relationship moving forward. Often in the process of arguing we're so overwhelmed we simply give up, become resentful, and are more distant, which can lead to unnecessary loss of the relationship. If we keep trying to have our voice heard in a reasonable manner, and encourage others to do so when we're calmer after separating, then it's likely that we're going to feel safer and connected, which is advantageous for us and fits with our programming (31-33).

That concludes the section on individual strategies for remediating our fear problem. There are dozens of other health and wellness practices I could recommend so that we have a more regulated mind and body; however, my goal was to be succinct and focus on the most concrete and impactful strategies that can help reverse our maladaptive coping and loss of intellectual honesty.

As I see it, the concepts discussed in this section (i.e., mindfulness, self check-in, and conflict resolution) are perhaps the most underutilized in Western culture, and, ironically, are the most challenging to implement. Please, feel free to incorporate as many other healthy, calming, compassionate, mindful, and understanding practices as you like into your fear management strategy.

I'm aware that I have not yet specifically addressed the four drivers of the fear problem discussed back in chapter 3. This section is not really devoted to addressing social phenomena. I would guess that a more mindful approach towards our use of social media/technology, our religious practices, and our finances could help lessen the stress and fear of our daily lives. These topics will be discussed in greater detail in the next section focused on cultural strategies for improving our fear problem.

Cultural Strategies

This section addressing the cultural level of fear hijacking might become challenging for you because I'm going to be proposing ideas and changes to how you function in your various tribes, which will inherently call into question some aspects of your self-identity. To be perfectly clear, I am in no way attempting to demean or defame with the statements and propositions forthcoming.

My hope is to provide very concrete challenges to the ideas underlying the three cultural level consequences: rigid tribalism, conflict, and violence. This section will be divided into two parts addressing how to reverse rigid tribalism and how to level off the conflict/violence consequences addressed in chapter 5.

Theoretically, addressing the tribalism consequence will impact the level of conflict and violence, so I will not specifically be addressing how to engage in less violent behavior. As I discussed in chapters 5 and 6, I believe that each level of consequences builds upon and exacerbates the previous level's consequences. In the same way, I believe our work at the individual level of fear management can bolster our success towards functioning more adaptively at the cultural level and will in turn prevent foolish and unnecessary violent behavior (e.g., religiously motivated violence, political protest violence, or gang violence).

As a final reminder, this is not an attempt to encourage you to give up your earthly possessions, abandon your phones and computers, give away your money, become anarchists, renounce your religious life, or return to a lifestyle reminiscent of the wandering mendicants of the Buddha's time or Plato's cave. I have done my best to avoid hyperbole and extremism and I will be focusing on a reasonable approach towards understanding and living out our tribalistic instincts.

Reversing Rigid Tribalism

I want to attack the problem of rigid tribalism on two fronts. First, I want to pitch to you an ideological shift about how to identify with your tribes. Secondarily, I want to encourage you to reflect on the degree of participation in your various tribes and the extent to which that could serve you in more or less adaptive ways. These are separate yet related goals and they need to be dealt with as such, separately and purposefully, because we all are functioning at various levels of commitment to our identities as members of tribes and living based upon the tribe's norms and values.

For example, some of you may be more rigid about your religious beliefs and heavily involved in religious practices. Others of you might see your religious identity more as a fraction of your identity and not its core, participating in rituals and services as you see fit without being overzealous or overinvolved. Finally, others of you—like the "cafeteria Catholic"—are far from involved or militarized and are not living based upon literal interpretations of your religious or holy books.

Regarding the notion of shifting and re-examining the extent to which we identify with our tribe, I think the simplest place to begin is to decide how useful it is to strongly identify with any of your given tribes. In chapter 5 I introduced the concept of adaptive group identification, which implies that we function best when the degree of group identification provides for better functioning and better chance of genetic survival.

The goal as I see it is to maintain a "sense" of identification with your tribe(s) in a manner that keeps you feeling connected, but also disconnected enough for you to feel free to function as an individual to pursue your life in a reasonable manner. My main problem, as discussed in chapter 5, is that when we over-identify with our tribe, then we start to lose our capacity to think critically and operate adaptively in our environment out of fear of rejection by our tribe.

This is the problem with preposterous phenomena observed in the U.S. nowadays like "identity politics" and religiously inspired violence seen in ISIS, in addition to many other smaller examples. If one's tribe, whether it is our racial group, family clan, religious group, hobby organization, career guild, or any other group to whom we belong hinders free thinking, exploration of life's mysteries, and autonomy, then there is a problem. This might seem to you as somewhat perplexing because, for instance, not every member or sub-group within a larger tribe can be radical or constricting in its ideology and expectations (i.e., one church of reasonable and loving people versus all members of the Catholic version of Christianity who adhere to harmful norms like avoiding birth control).

In order to develop adaptive group identification, I think we need to have rational expectations about how we identify and understand ourselves as creatures walking across this planet. The best example in modern history is Martin Luther King, Jr.'s "I have a dream" speech containing the famous line:

"I have a dream that my four little children will one day live in a nation where they will not be judged by the color of their skin, but by the content of their character."

We still have not figured out that our sense of identity is fluid and we cling to facets of how we choose to identify, such as our skin color, our 23rd chromosome, our sexual orientation, our religious preferences, or our country of origin, like an infant to a blanket.

I challenge you to ask yourself a few very simple questions regarding any tribe that you currently participate in either literally (e.g., family relationships) or more metaphorically (i.e., "I'm a black man" or "I'm gay"). First ask yourself this: "How important, how crucial for my survival, is it for me to identify this way?" How you answer that question will influence your answer to the second question: "Does my identification as _____ allow me to *feel* free to relate to others who are/ seem different?" If you answered the second question and are struggling to feel free, then I suggest stepping back from this piece of your self-understanding and moving towards a more integrative way of seeing yourself (i.e., lessening the extent to which this piece of your identity puzzle affects how you see yourself and conduct yourself).

We are not simple creatures, and living as if we are only men or only straight is a boring and empty life. Many facets of how we self-identify are not within our control (i.e., skin color or 23rd chromosome), yet others are. To be fair, different people from different regions on this planet will struggle with the first question more because, for instance, in many countries within the Middle East, if you are not identifying with the correct religious group, then your chances of dying are great...and if you try to leave your family's religion, you can be killed. Here in the United States, we have a much freer society, so we have more choice. I propose that we take advantage of what freedoms we have to better function.

Regarding the degree of participation in your various tribes, I want to center this discussion on two things: how big our tribes are and how consistently we have interpersonal contact with others in our tribe. The first challenge is figuring out how many people we really "need" to survive and thrive. I think that given how much society has advanced and how much contact we have with others nowadays, we likely need to shrink our relationship circles.

Obviously, having close relationships is highly beneficial to our health and welfare (34-45), but I think we're oversaturated. This leaves us with a problem of figuring out whom to keep in our lives, what metric should we use to evaluate the importance of keeping people involved in our lives, and to what extent. The most scientific approach to this question that makes sense to me is based upon the work of Robin Dunbar.

Dunbar conducted decades of anthropology and psychology research focusing on brain complexity and norms across cultures and species, which has resulted in "Dunbar's number," an estimate of the maximum number of people/relationships we can reasonably manage. According to Dunbar, that number is about 150. To be fair, some have challenged Dunbar's number (46, 47) whereas others have sought to expand upon or confirm the concept (48-52).

Dunbar's original work (53, 54) hypothesized that, because of our brain's functional capacity, humans can process information and manage feelings for about 150 people/relationships optimally, which are divided into four types of relationship groups that are envisioned as four concentric circles. The innermost layer, or smallest circle, is composed of the five closest/deepest relationships one can have (e.g., parents or romantic partners). The second largest circle contains 10 relatively close relationships (e.g., more distal family relationships and close friends/colleagues). The third largest circle contains 35 people of mild to moderate intimacy and familiarity (e.g., neighbors and other familiar conspecifics), and the final layer is approximately 100 people from our past/present with whom we are familiar but whose relationships do not require intense participation (e.g., a friend from school whom you see at reunions and on trips home). This is the basic landscape of optimal relational functional capacity, and I think it can be nicely applied to our current circumstances to help ease rigid tribalism.

I believe that many people in Western cultures like the U.S. might participate in either too many tribes, which would automatically force us to keep in contact with well over 150 people, or we participate with too many members of one or more tribes in our life in unnecessarily intense ways, or perhaps both problematic dynamics are affecting you.

The simple example is how we engage in social media. Of the approximately 1 billion people on Facebook, the average user has somewhere between 155 (55) and 388 (56) "friends." Obviously, the extent to which these "friends" are more intense and connected with the user is up for debate and unknowable. Automatically, however, the average Facebook user is well over Dunbar's number. Now, imagine how many other people not associated with Facebook are involved in the average person's life.

Maybe one or two dozen other people, family or friends? In this way, we're overwhelming our capacity to process all the intricacies and anxieties of having relationships. I cannot imagine a way in which having more people in our life will result in less fear. Now, apply this same logic to those of you involved in a religious belief system.

In addition to your family, coworkers, friends, lovers (etc.) that do not attend your church, roughly 46 percent of you attend a church of 100 people or fewer, and 37 percent attend a church with between 100-499 people. Simply by practicing a religious belief system, we automatically are over Dunbar's number (57). You could take this logic system (i.e., number of people in tribal group + number of people outside tribal group = beyond 150 people) and apply it to many common groups in which we participate nowadays (i.e., political, religious, cultural, hobbies, etc.).

If my basic logic is correct about Dunbar's number and how many people we interact with every day, week, month, and year, then I believe there are two simple—not easy—solutions to our tribe participation problem resulting in fear. First, maybe we should limit the number of people we interact with.

Do you honestly need to interact with hundreds or even thousands of people on Twitter, Facebook, Instagram, or Snapchat? Imagine if you took all of the emotional and cognitive energy expended by participating in social media and invested it into your relationships in the here and now that really matter (i.e., lovers, close friends, close colleagues, etc.)—in a manner more fitting with how we're designed, not what's popular or what feels good.

Secondarily, I believe we need to limit the number of tribes in which we participate. It is common and more than understandable to want to feel included by various groups sharing similar ideologies or customs. For example, maybe your nuclear family is the most toxic tribe (i.e., most rigid about beliefs and emotionally unhealthy), and it would be wise to pull away from them. For others, maybe you belong to polarized or violent political/ideological groups and need to leave them.

Regardless of whether the group is professional or personal, the groups in which you participate that are the most rigid, most polarizing, most closed off to change or free thought, these are the groups that are causing both the most societal harm as well as personal harm to you and your intellectual/emotional freedom—exacerbating the fear problem. Even if you leave a few ideological groups, you still have a voice, you still "belong," and you have numerous opportunities in your other tribes and in your close relationships to feel seen and attempt to enact change through expression of free thought.

This may seem like an overly simplistic approach to combating rigid tribalism, but it stands to reason that we operate in very simple and patterned ways. What the cultural level of the fear problem comes down to is an inability to reform tribes to operate more logically or an inability to have intergroup harmony.

One of the fundamental problems with tribalism is that it is so deeply programmed into our psyche and engrained in the social mores of our cultures/families that we don't notice it working in the background as we wander through our daily lives (58, 59). So, step one is acknowledging that our tribe or ideological group is struggling with rigidity, closed-mindedness, or violence.

Step two is examining your allegiance to your tribe and if it's really all that necessary to identify with said tribe to survive both literally and socially (i.e., advance socially). Step three is to reflect on steps one and two and make a strategic decision about how often or intensely you involve yourself with various groups, or simply leave some groups. This will help us get in fewer fights over ideology and allow us to pare down our social group somewhere closer to Dunbar's number.

Global Strategies

The final layer of the fear problem relates to geopolitical dynamics. The two consequences of the fear problem at the global level I discussed in the previous chapter were loss of trust and faster-moving societies, and the focus here for me will be rebuilding trust. The best metaphor for global society is business in my opinion, so I'm going to pull predominantly from research related to the fields of economics and industrial-organizational psychology to describe some tips for our world leaders, or for those of you reading who can in some way influence world leaders through personal or political means.

Again, I'm not an international scholar or any kind of expert on geopolitical affairs, so the tips below are simply what I perceive to be reasonable goals or aspirational principles. As always, I welcome criticism and debate. This will also be the shortest section because it is the furthest outside my wheelhouse and least likely to change because of the billions of variables involved. I think it's going to be nearly impossible for global society to slow down to a more mindful pace because modern economic systems, technologies, and military actions are not designed to move slowly anymore; however, I would like to believe that we can maybe pull back the throttle a little with some changes.

The first tip is kind of a "no duh" idea: to focus our policies and energies on building trust. Trust is essential to running businesses and playing well with allies as well as competitors (60-62). The two qualities of leaders that seem to engender trust are reciprocity and responsiveness (63), so global leaders and other key players might reflect on to what extent they embody those qualities. Moreover, it seems like a smaller number of alliances, like in the discussion about tribalism and Dunbar's number earlier, would be helpful for maintaining trust and optimal international dynamics (64).

With fewer allies, that would likely slow down geopolitical relations and make it easier to form a deeper relationship with allied government officials—theoretically. Finally, people seem to have a problem with corrupt governments, so it stands to reason that we should do our best to support more transparent governments and do our best to discourage and distance ourselves from corrupt leaders (65, 66). These are the most reasonable strategies I can foresee impacting the global climate in a positive direction, and they hopefully will play a part in diminishing our fear problem.

The Four Drivers

To end this book, I want to keep good on my promise and talk about how to incorporate all the potential solutions from earlier in this chapter as a means of beginning to unravel the four drivers of our fear phenomenon discussed in chapter 3. This will be brief because I believe these four phenomena (i.e., technology, politics, religion, and greed) are so enormous and so complex in scope that no simple solution could exist.

Regarding technology, I think there are two attitudes we can adopt to reclaim our peace of mind: mindfulness and skepticism. As I alluded to in chapter 3, we have become engrossed by the various forms of technology used every day in countries like the U.S. to the point where people need "detoxes" from their smartphone or social media application. If we adopt a more mindful attitude about our technology, then maybe we can develop a slower approach to relating and refocus on person-to-person connection in a more meaningful manner.

Secondarily, I think we need to keep a skeptical eye on the potential perils of technological advancement and overreliance on technology to make life "easier" or "better." Recently, a great deal of discussion has occurred regarding topics like artificial intelligence (i.e., AI) (67) and genetic editing using technology like "CRISPR." Countries like the U.S. have the luxury of transparency in news media and research journals, and the more informed we are as consumers about controversial and potentially life-threatening or culture-modifying technology like AI and gene editing, the better chance we have for survival.

Regarding politics, there simply is so much to say and I already offered some thoughts in the global solutions section earlier in this chapter;

however, I'll refer to the mindfulness, intellectual honesty, and tribalism arguments above because I think they could serve best to reduce the problem of political insanity observed in the U.S. and abroad. The incessant arguing, mud-slinging, and operating in an "us-versus-them" manner is creating insanity and fear like never before, in the U.S. especially.

We need to breathe. We need to stop and think before we speak. We need to all challenge our perspectives. We need to let go of politically partisan thinking. We need to start judging ideas for their merit and stop agreeing or disagreeing with them based upon who says them, or because of the speaker's political ideology.

This tribalistic and automatic response we have against people who adhere to different beliefs and ideas is not going to end because that's just human nature; however, we can reel it back in a little by challenging how intellectually honest we are when we debate and by breathing before we act. We need to be informed consumers, not people reacting because of sound bites espoused by news anchors or politicians. The more mindful we are, the less rigid we are. The more mindful we are, the more critically we can think.

Regarding religion, I challenge you to consider the extent to which your beliefs make sense and the extent to which they contribute to a rigidly tribalistic lifestyle. As I mentioned in chapter 3, this is not an atheist manifesto. For the atheist argument that picks apart various religions and their flaws, please refer to the works of authors like Sam Harris, Christopher Hitchens, Daniel Dennett, Richard Dawkins, Steven Pinker, Edward Wilson, Lawrence Krauss, and Peter Singer—to name a few.

I'm here to argue about the consequences of your beliefs and practices. The more that your beliefs and rituals cause *you* to create rigidity and disconnection with others, then the more problematic the belief is. If your belief in a god or god(s) compel you to inhibit the freedom of others or cause harm, that's a problem.

For example, a Buddhist may adhere to unscientific beliefs about Karma and reincarnation, but the other tenets espoused in the 8-fold path are rarely, if ever, going to compel a Buddhist monk to cause harm to others. Try the two-step process for reversing rigid tribalism mentioned above and give Socratic thinking a try. If we continue to operate with our heads in the sand because we're afraid of what will happen if we challenge our religious beliefs, then more groups like ISIS will arise and more intergroup conflict will arise.

Regarding greed, I believe we must focus on combatting fear at the individual and cultural level first. Some of the problems that cultivate greed can be affected by bigger forces (i.e., governments and private economic institutions), and some of the problems must be addressed by individuals—like our fears of failure, success, shame, feeling "oppressed," addiction, mental health issues, and other facets of the fear problem that create a desire for greed or a lifestyle that can only end in poverty.

First, we need to admit the truth of reality, the normal curve of life. Second, we need to breathe and make more rational decisions about personal and collective finances. There are many wealthy individuals who are causing minimal harm in this world, and they do not need to be demonized using tribalistic and intellectually dishonest rhetoric like "one percenter."

This accomplishes nothing and creates more harm and more of a divide. Moreover, some people are going to struggle more than others, some people will financially struggle more than others because of a combination of both personal and sociopolitical reasons, and we *need* to accept that because equality does not exist anywhere in nature (i.e., normal curve).

This notion of equality is an artificial and aspirational construct of human thought born out of existential fear, I assert. Once we accept this and breathe a little, then we can make more reasonable decisions for ourselves as individuals about being financially responsible, learning how to save, how to work harder, and learning how to sacrifice some of our wants and needs for the sake of future success.

Many authors since the time of Epictetus, spanning everything from philosophy to civil rights, from Kierkegaard to Martin Luther King, Jr., tell us that we need to struggle as individuals and as cultures to achieve a better outcome for ourselves. In the U.S. specifically, there are many variables to our fear-driven greed and economic issues.

Final Thoughts

At the start of this book, I set out with the goals of showing you that our fear is getting out of control, why that's so, some of the problems we face because of it, and some solutions to help reverse the fear problem. I hope that you feel as if I've accomplished those goals. Furthermore, I hope you understand how diligently I have worked to hedge when I'm uncertain, support my ideas with credible sources, and operate from a place of logic and not rhetoric. Some of my biases show here, and that's fine.

Over the course of the past year or so researching and writing this book, much in my life and in the U.S. where I live has changed, and I think any shifts in my tone reflect changes I experienced—while still staying true to principles like intellectual honesty and transparency. I wanted this to feel like a dialogue rather than a professor spouting statistics to you in a classroom. Most of all, I wanted this to make sense because it probably feels like much of what's happening in the world today does not seem to make much sense at all.

We are at a crossroads as individuals, cultures, and a global community. With how much we know about human functioning and wellbeing, we have a decision to make. In fact, I see that there are only two choices. Choice number one: we choose to continue operating on automatic pilot and living a fear-driven reactionary lifestyle, which means we have chosen—I believe—to keep suffering unnecessarily. Choice number two: we choose to work on the fear problem, live a more mindful life, reason more honestly, and live as we were designed to live, which means society has a chance of not eventually destroying itself. Our personal success and wellbeing is at stake, as is the welfare of those we love and those with whom we live and work. What will you choose?

REFERENCES

1. Rock, D., Siegel, D.J., Poelmans, S.A.Y., & Payne, J. (2012). The healthy mind platter. *NeuroLeadership Journal, 4*, 1-23.

2. Xu, M., Purdon, C., Seli, P., & Smilek, D. (2017). Mindfulness and mind wandering: The protective effects of brief meditation in anxious individuals. *Consciousness and Cognition, 51*, 157-165. https://doi.org/10.1016/j.concog.2017.03.009

3. Arch, J. J., Wolitzky-Taylor, K. B., Eifert, G. H., & Craske M. G. (2012). Longitudinal treatment mediation of traditional cognitive behavioral therapy and acceptance and commitment therapy for anxiety disorders. *Behaviour Research and Therapy, 50*, 469–478.

4. Beauchemin, J., Hutchins, T. L., & Patterson, F. (2008). Mindfulness meditation may lessen anxiety, promote social skills, and improve academic performance among adolescents with learning disabilities. *Complementary Health Practice Review, 13*(1), 34-45.

5. Evans, S., Ferrando, S., Findler, M., Stowell, C., Smart, C., & Haglin, D. (2008). Mindfulness-based cognitive therapy for generalized anxiety disorder. *Journal of Anxiety Disorders, 22*(4), 716-721.

6. Hofmann, S. G., Sawyer, A. T., Witt, A. A., & Oh, D. (2010). The effect of mindfulness-based therapy on anxiety and depression: a meta-analytic review. *Journal of Consulting and Clinical Psychology, 78*(2), 169-183.

7. Marchand, W. R. (2012). Mindfulness-based stress reduction, mindfulness-based cognitive therapy, and zen meditation for depression, anxiety, pain, and psychological distress. *Journal of Psychiatric Practice®, 18*(4), 233-252.

8. Sears, S., & Kraus, S. (2009). I Think Therefore I Om: Cognitive Distortions and Coping Style as Mediators for the Effects of Mindfulness Meditation on Anxiety, Positive and Negative Affect, and Hope. *Journal of Clinical Psychology, 65*(6), 561-573.

9. Vollestad, J., Nielsen, M.B. & Nielsen, G.H. (2012). Mindfulness- and acceptance-based interventions for anxiety disorders: A systematic review and meta-analysis. *British Journal of Clinical Psychology, 51*(3), 239-260. https:/ 10.1111/j.2044-8260.2011.02024.x

10. Zeidan, F., Johnson, S. K., Diamond, B. J., David, Z., & Goolkasian, P. (2010). Mindfulness meditation improves cognition: Evidence of brief mental training. *Consciousness and Cognition, 19*(2), 597-605.

11. Zeidan, F., Martucci, K. T., Kraft, R. A., McHaffie, J. G., & Coghill, R. C. (2013). Neural correlates of mindfulness meditation-related anxiety relief. *Social Cognitive and Affective Neuroscience, 9*(6), 751-759.

12. Gapp, K., Bohacek, J., Grossmann, J., Brunner, A.M., Manuella, F., Nanni, P., Mansuy, I.M. (2016). Potential of Environmental Enrichment to Prevent Transgenerational Effects of Paternal Trauma. *Neuropsychopharmacology, 41*, 2749–2758; doi:10.1038/npp.2016.87.

13. Yehuda, Rachel et al. (2015). Holocaust exposure induced intergenerational effects on FKBP5 methylation. *Biological Psychiatry*, *80*(5), 372 - 380.

14. McGowan, P.O. (2013). Epigenomic mechanisms of early adversity and HPA dysfunction: considerations for PTSD research. *Front Psychiatry* 4:110. doi:10.3389/fpsyt.2013.00110

15. Callaghan BL, Graham B, Li S, Richardson R. (2013). From resilience to vulnerability: mechanistic insights into the effects of stress on transitions in critical period plasticity. *Front Psychiatry* 4:90. doi:10.3389/fpsyt.2013.00090.

16. Maddox SA, Schafe GE, Ressler KJ. (2013). Exploring epigenetic regulation of fear memory and biomarkers associated with post-traumatic stress disorder. *Front Psychiatry* 4:62. doi:10.3389/fpsyt.2013.00062.

17. Ducci, F., & Goldman, D. (2012). The Genetic Basis of Addictive Disorders. *The Psychiatric Clinics of North America*, *35*(2), 495–519. http://doi.org/10.1016/j.psc.2012.03.010

18. Kosfeld, M., Heinrichs, M., Zak, P. J., Fischbacher, U., & Fehr, E. (2005). Oxytocin increases trust in humans. *Nature*, *435*(7042), 673-676.

19. Witkiewitz, K., Bowen, S., Harrop, E. N., Douglas, H., Enkema, M., & Sedgwick, C. (2014). Mindfulness-Based Treatment to Prevent Addictive Behavior Relapse: Theoretical Models and Hypothesized Mechanisms of Change. *Substance Use & Misuse*, *49*(5), 513–524. http://doi.org/10.3109/10826084.2014.891845

20. Garland, E. L., Froeliger, B., & Howard, M. O. (2013). Mindfulness Training Targets Neurocognitive Mechanisms of Addiction at the Attention-Appraisal-Emotion Interface. *Frontiers in Psychiatry*, *4*, 173. http://doi.org/10.3389/fpsyt.2013.00173

21. Witkiewitz, K., Marlatt, G. A., & Walker, D. (2005). Mindfulness-based relapse prevention for alcohol and substance use disorders. *Journal of Cognitive Psychotherapy*, *19*(3), 211-228.

22. Guenin, L.M. (2005). Intellectual honesty. *Synthese*, *145*, 177-232.

23. Rahmani, P. & Moheb, N. (2010). The effectiveness of clay therapy and narrative therapy on anxiety of pre-school children: a comparative study, *Procedia - Social and Behavioral Sciences*, *5*,23-27, doi.org/10.1016/j.sbspro.2010.07.044.

24. Malone, C. Forbat, L., Robb, M., & Seden, J. (2004). Externalizing the Problem. In M. White & D. Epston (eds.), *Relating Experiences: Stories from health and social care*. New York, NY: Routledge.

25. University of California - Los Angeles. (2007, June 22). Putting Feelings Into Words Produces Therapeutic Effects In The Brain. ScienceDaily. Retrieved May 8, 2016 from www.sciencedaily.com/releases/2007/06/070622090727.htm

26. Frith, C. (2013). The psychology of volition. *Experimental Brain Research*, *229*(3), 289-299. doi:10.1007/s00221-013-3407-6

27. Antai-Otong, D. (2001). Creative Stress-Management Techniques For Self-Renewal. *Dermatology Nursing*, *13*(1), 31-39.

28. Siegel, D.J. (2011). *Mindsight: The New Science of Personal Transformation*. New York, NY: Bantam Books.

29.   Hülsheger, U.R., Alberts, H. J. E. M., Feinholdt, A., Lang, J. W. B. (2013). Benefits of mindfulness at work: The role of mindfulness in emotion regulation, emotional exhaustion, and job satisfaction. *Journal of Applied Psychology*, *98*(2), 310-325. http://dx.doi.org/10.1037/a0031313

30.   Roemer, L., Lee, J.K., Salters-Pedneault, K., Erisman, S.M., Orsillo, S.M., Mennin, D.S. (2009). Mindfulness and emotion regulation difficulties in generalized anxiety disorder: Preliminary evidence for independent and overlapping contributions. *Behavior Therapy*, *40*(2), 142-154.

31.   Siegel, D.J. (2012). *Pocket guide to interpersonal neurobiology: An integrative handbook of the mind.* New York: W.W. Norton & Company.

32.   Hasse Walum, et al. (2008). Genetic variation in the vasopressin receptor 1a gene (AVPR1A) associates with pair-bonding behavior in humans. *Proceedings of the National Academy of Sciences*, *105*(37) 14153-14156

33.   Panksepp, J. (1998). *Affective Neuroscience: The Foundations of Human and Animal Emotions.* New York: Oxford University Press.

34.   Barclay, P. (2016). Biological markets and the effects of partner choice on cooperation and friendship. *Current Opinion in Psychology*, *7*, 33-38.

35.   Brennan, A. A., & Enns, J. T. (2015). When two heads are better than one: Interactive Versus Independent Benefits of Collaborative Cognition. *Psychonomic Bulletin & Review*, *22*(4), 1076-1082.

36.   Epstein, J. L., & Karweit, N. (Eds.). (2014). *Friends in school: Patterns of selection and influence in secondary schools.* Elsevier.

37.   Fitzpatrick, S., & Bussey, K. (2014). The role of perceived friendship self-efficacy as a protective factor against the negative effects of social victimization. *Social Development*, *23*(1), 41-60.

38.   Goodenow, C., & Grady, K. E. (1993). The relationship of school belonging and friends' values to academic motivation among urban adolescent students. *The Journal of Experimental Education*, *62*(1), 60-71.

39.   Graham, S., Munniksma, A., & Juvonen, J. (2014). Psychosocial benefits of cross-ethnic friendships in urban middle schools. *Child Development*, *85*(2), 469-483.

40.   Ladd, G. W. (1990). Having friends, keeping friends, making friends, and being liked by peers in the classroom: Predictors of children's early school adjustment? *Child Development*, *61*(4), 1081-1100.

41.   Lakon, C. M., Wang, C., Butts, C. T., Jose, R., Timberlake, D. S., & Hipp, J. R. (2015). A dynamic model of adolescent friendship networks, parental influences, and smoking. *Journal of Youth and Adolescence*, *44*(9), 1767-1786.

42.   Myers, D. G. (2000). The Funds, Friends, and Faith of Happy People. *American Psychologist*, *55*(1), 56.

43.   Owen, J., Fincham, F. D., & Manthos, M. (2013). Friendship after a friends with benefits relationship: deception, psychological functioning, and social connectedness. *Archives of Sexual Behavior*, *42*(8), 1443-1449.

44.   Ryan, R. M., Stiller, J. D., & Lynch, J. H. (1994). Representations of relationships to teachers,

parents, and friends as predictors of academic motivation and self-esteem. *The Journal of Early Adolescence, 14*(2), 226-249.

45.   Pietromaonaco, P.R. & Collins, N.L. (2017). Interpersonal mechanisms linking close relationships to health. *American Psychologist, 72*(6), 531-542.

46.   Wellman, B. (2012). Is Dunbar's number up?. *British Journal of Psychology, 103*(2), 174-176.

47.   De Ruiter, J., Weston, G., & Lyon, S. M. (2011). Dunbar's number: group size and brain physiology in humans reexamined. *American Anthropologist, 113*(4), 557-568.

48.   Brashears, M. E. (2013). Humans use Compression Heuristics to Improve the Recall of Social Networks. *Scientific Reports, 3*, 1513. http://doi.org/10.1038/srep01513

49.   Gonçalves, B., Perra, N., & Vespignani, A. (2011). Modeling users' activity on twitter networks: Validation of Dunbar's number. *PloS one, 6*(8), e22656.

50.   Bliss, C. A., Kloumann, I. M., Harris, K. D., Danforth, C. M., & Dodds, P. S. (2012). Twitter reciprocal reply networks exhibit assortativity with respect to happiness. *Journal of Computational Science, 3*(5), 388-397.

51.   Dunbar, R. (2012). Social Networks: Human Social Networks. *New Scientist, 214*(2859), iv-v.

52.   Von Der Heide, R., Vyas, G., & Olson, I.R. (2014). The social network-network: size is predicted by brain structure and function in the amygdala and paralimbic regions. *Social Cognitive and Affective Neuroscience, 9*(12), 1962–1972, https://doi.org/10.1093/scan/nsu009

53.   Dunbar, R.I. (1993). Coevolution of neocortical size, group size and language in humans. *Behavioral and Brain Sciences, 16*(4), 681-693.

54.   Dunbar, R. I. (1998). The Social Brain Hypothesis. *Brain, 9*(10), 178-190.

55.   Knapton, S. (2016). Facebook users have 155 friends-but would trust just 4 in a crisis. The Telegraph. Retrieved on August 28th, 2017 from: http://www.telegraph.co.uk/news/science/science-news/12108412/Facebook-users-have-155-friends-but-would-trust-just-four-in-a-crisis.html

56.   Smith, K. (2016). Marketing: 47 Incredible Facebook Statistics. Brandwatch. Retrieved on August 28th, 2017 from: https://www.brandwatch.com/blog/47-facebook-statistics-2016/

57.   Barna Group. (2016). The state of the Church 2016. Research Releases in Faith & Christianity. Retrieved on August 28th, 2017 from: https://www.barna.com/research/state-church-2016/

58.   McDonald, M. M., Navarrete, C. D., & Van Vugt, M. (2012). Evolution and the psychology of intergroup conflict: the male warrior hypothesis. Philosophical Transactions of the Royal Society B: Biological Sciences, *367*(1589), 670–679. http://doi.org/10.1098/rstb.2011.0301

59.   Wilson, E. O. (2013). Evolution and our inner conflict. *The Journal of General Education, 62*(1), 3-6.

60.   Parkhe, A. (1998). Building trust in international alliances. *Journal of World Business, 33*(4), 417-437.

61.   Boersma, M. F., Buckley, P. J., & Ghauri, P. N. (2003). Trust in international joint venture relationships. *Journal of Business Research, 56*(12), 1031-1042.

62. Friman, M., Gärling, T., Millett, B., Mattsson, J., & Johnston, R. (2002). An analysis of international business-to-business relationships based on the Commitment–Trust theory. *Industrial Marketing Management, 31*(5), 403-409.

63. Kelman, H. C. (2005). Building trust among enemies: The central challenge for international conflict resolution. *International Journal of Intercultural Relations, 29*(6), 639-650.

64. Robson, M. J., Katsikeas, C. S., & Bello, D. C. (2008). Drivers and performance outcomes of trust in international strategic alliances: The role of organizational complexity. *Organization Science, 19*(4), 647-665.

65. Rothstein, B. (2011). *The Quality of Government: Corruption, Social Trust, and Inequality in International Perspective.* Chicago, IL: University of Chicago Press.

66. Rothstein, B. (2013). Corruption and social trust: Why the Fish Rots from the Head Down. *Social Research, 80*(4), 1009-1032.

67. Future of Life Institute. (2017). Benefits & risks of artificial intelligence. Retrieved on August 18th, 2017 from: https://futureoflife.org/background/benefits-risks-of-artificial-intelligence/

FURTHER READING

Helpful Links

Wellness:

drdansiegel.com/resources/healthy_mind_platter

shcs.ucdavis.edu/wellness/what-is-wellness

samhsa.gov/wellness-initiative/eight-dimensions-wellness

globalwellnessinstitute.org

Free Guided Meditations:

marc.ucla.edu/mindful-meditations

tarabrach.com/guided-meditations

chopra.com/articles/guided-meditations

Books on Mindfulness

Kornfield, J. (1998). *Meditation for Beginners*. Denver, CO: Sounds True Publishing

Kabat-Zinn, J. (2013). *Full catastrophe living: Using the wisdom of your body and mind to face stress, pain, and illness.* (2nd, Ed.), Revised and Updated. New York, NY: Bantam/Random House Publishing.

Kabat-Zinn, J. (2012). *Mindfulness for Beginners: Reclaiming the Present Moment—and Your Life.* Denver, CO: Sounds True Publishing.

Nhat-Hahn, T. (1999). *The Miracle of Mindfulness: An Introduction to the Practice of Meditation.* Boston, MA: Beacon Press.

Siegel, D.J. (2007). *The Mindful Brain: Reflection and Attunement in the Cultivation of Well-Being.* New York: W.W. Norton & Company.

Books on Socratic Questioning, Intellectual Honesty, and Critical Thinking:

De Botton, A. (2000). *The Consolations of Philosophy*. London, UK: Hamish Hamilton.

Kahneman, D. (2011). *Thinking, Fast and Slow*. New York, NY: Farrar, Strauss and Giroux.

Kreeft, P. (2010). *Socratic logic: A Logic Text Using Socratic Method, Platonic Questions, and Aristotelian Principles.* (3rd ed.) Dougherty, T. (Ed.). Southbend, IN: St. Augustine's Press.

Sagan, Carl (March 1997). *The Demon-Haunted World: Science As a Candle in the Dark* (Paperback ed.). New York, NY: Ballantine Books.

Shermer, M. (2002). *Why People Believe Weird Things: Pseudoscience, Superstition, and Other Confusions of Our Time*. New York, NY: Holt Paperbacks.

ABOUT THE AUTHOR

Dr. Patrick Lockwood holds a Doctorate of Psychology and has extensive experience working with addictions, trauma, and personality disorders. He has worked at every level of the mental health and addiction treatment industries throughout his doctoral education and post-graduate employment experiences.

Patrick currently serves as a therapist at a treatment center in Malibu focusing on comorbid trauma and addiction, where he also spends time on developing scientific presentations to increase awareness of science-driven solutions for mental health and addiction issues at conferences and community events. He also works as a business consultant in the Los Angeles area for both non-profit and for-profit businesses focused on mental health, addiction, and social issues.

The inspiration for *The Fear Problem* began prior to the 2016 election when Patrick began to notice the ever-increasing disconnect between people when it came to topics such as religion, politics, wealth, and other "isms" (i.e., racism, sexism, and heterosexism, among others). So, Patrick set out to research and understand the complex matrix of psychological, biological, evolutionary, and social forces that seemed to have pushed humanity into factions at war and, more importantly, attempt to find practical solutions to it.

When he's not consulting, working with patients, or writing, he enjoys physical fitness activities—he is a regular at the gym, enjoys working on cars, and plays the guitar in his spare time. He currently resides in the Los Angeles area with his fiancé.

The Fear Problem is Dr. Lockwood's first book of many to come, so be on the lookout for future titles!